Also by Governor Robert L. Ehrlich, Jr.

America: Hope for Change

Bet You Didn't See That One Coming: Obama, Trump, and the End of Washington's Regular Order

Original, Unconventional & Inconvenient: Donald J. Trump and His MAGA Movement

Advance Praise for *142 Ways America Went from Sweet Land of Liberty to Weak, Woke, and Wobbly*

"The bottom line is that Ehrlich's bottom lines tell us an awful lot about what's been awful in Joe Biden's America—and he brings the receipts!"

—Ken Cuccinelli, 46th Attorney General of Virginia (2010–2014), Acting Director of the United States Citizenship and Immigration Services (2019–2021)

"...Governor Ehrlich comes through with another masterpiece. This one is the definitive reference book and 'how-to' manual as the nation prepares for the critical battles of 2024."

—Charlie Gerow, Former Vice Chair, American Conservative Union

"This is a perfectly timed good and bad ideas book by freedom-loving Gov. Bob Ehrlich. He's (Bob, The Gov) thoughtfully compiled issues, policies, and principles that all voters should seriously consider when determining the helpful agenda to make our USA a competitively prosperous, much safer, better educated, and more affordable country in which to live, learn, work, and raise our families."

—George Allen, Former Virginia Governor and U.S. Senator

"Governor Ehrlich demonstrates the same common-sense conservatism that he displayed as he successfully applied conservative principles to deep blue Maryland in the 2000s. This compendium of indictments against the Biden administration's wholesale attack on America's economy, values, national security, and sovereignty serves as a reminder both for voters and any incoming GOP administration of the damage which has been done and pillars of freedom which must be restored. Truly a must-read for everyone who cares about America as a future beacon of hope for the world."

—Richard Manning, President,
Americans for Limited Government

"In this significant work, Governor Ehrlich persuasively details why and how a more conservative perspective on America's critical issues can solve those issues and at the same time reduce the polarization that is wracking America. He spares no criticism of the Biden administration's failures on the economy, crime, education, immigration, and foreign policy—but also takes the GOP to task when its rhetoric does not match up to its action."

—Richard Vatz, PhD, Towson
University Distinguished Professor

"A timely and convenient reference guide—full of useful facts—that makes the case against the Biden administration's onslaught…must-reading for undecided voters."

—David McIntosh,
President, Club for Growth

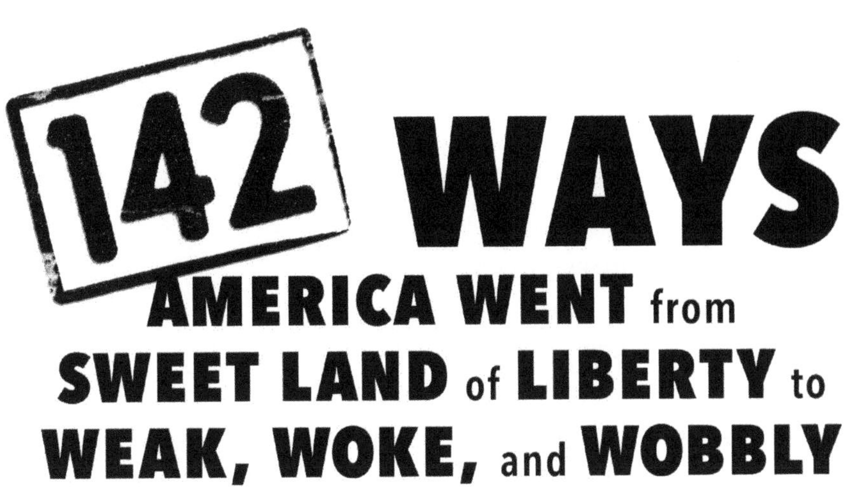

A REFERENCE GUIDE TO THE BIDEN YEARS

GOVERNOR BOB EHRLICH

A POST HILL PRESS BOOK
ISBN: 979-8-88845-915-7
ISBN (eBook): 979-8-88845-917-1

142 Ways America Went from Sweet Land of Liberty to Weak, Woke, and Wobbly:
A Reference Guide to the Biden Years
© 2024 by Governor Bob Ehrlich
All Rights Reserved

Post Hill Press
New York • Nashville
posthillpress.com

Published in the United States of America
1 2 3 4 5 6 7 8 9 10

To my incredible family, with lots
of love. No son, husband, or father
could be more fortunate.

CONTENTS

Chapter 10: Institutions

Chapter 11: Race

Chapter 12: Speech

INTRODUCTION

The Biden era has marked numerous low points in American politics, but one small story is symbolic: The sitting president of the United States appeared to nod off while mumbling during a high-profile Oval Office meeting with Israeli President Isaac Herzog. That the resulting embarrassment was glossed over by the legacy media says all you need to know about how the fourth estate has been running cover for Joe Biden and his administration.

With rare exceptions, the media sees itself as having a singular mission: To ensure the orange menace from Queens is never again provided the opportunity to occupy the White House. And so—even if it means a bum's-rush coverage of serious events, or simply refusing to report on the latest cognitive miscue by the president—any storyline that damages the Biden presidency is sure to be minimized or buried.

Not that any of the foregoing breaks new ground, but 2023 brought many elements of the Biden era together for me. The inflationary spiral of 2022 spiked again in the summer of 2023 and had the Federal Reserve signaling extended higher interest rates. Up to ten million migrants had taken Mr. Biden up on his open-borders invitation. Fentanyl from Mexican labs was killing record numbers of America's young people. The long-awaited Durham report had illustrated the extent to which a disturbing level of political censorship had reached senior levels at the Department of Justice. The Twitter and Facebook files reflected the extent to which nearly a dozen government agencies had threatened, cajoled, and lobbied social media platforms to censor news that did not comport with Biden-approved narratives. Then there were daily reports about how Hunter Biden had "earned" all that foreign money while his dad occupied the two most powerful positions on earth. Adding insult to injury, the immensely popular Tucker Carlson was unceremoniously removed from his prime-time spot on Fox News for reasons still unknown.

One repercussion in the Ehrlich household was less time spent watching Fox News, despite our affinity for Sean Hannity, Jesse Watters, Laura Ingraham, Trace Gallagher and Bret Baier. *Someone* had to make a stand against the media establishment. In light of subsequent ratings, millions had similar thoughts.

Back to the genesis of this effort. As summer turned to fall and fall to winter, an aggressive GOP House was able to shine a bright light on Hunter's laptop, the continuing collusion between Big Tech and Big Government, the shockingly politi-cized Biden Department of Justice that had quietly approved a sweetheart plea deal for the benefit of the younger Biden before being exposed by a federal judge, and the spectacularly dys-functional series of foreign policy miscalculations that weak-ened America while strengthening China, Russia, and Iran on the world stage.

I accordingly began to update my Lincoln Day Dinner stump speech on all the things that had gone wrong since January 2021. Not an easy task. Here, ten items turned into thirty items and then sixty and ninety and more. Every day seemed to produce another chapter of either woke-gone-mad or simple negligence gone askew—and almost always to the detriment of Americans who wear blue collars and who have become objects of scorn for our highly educated bicoastal elites. In the process, that good ol' American dream seemed to be slipping away.

That wonderful dream is now in official jeopardy—a state of affairs brought to you by a myriad of failed policy initiatives from Washington, D.C.

All of which has led to this call to arms—or at least a list of grievances. Each Biden-era incident or policy is categorized for easy reference and is also condensed for the reader's convenience. It is hoped this "reference guide" approach will make it easier for the political warrior within you to engage in a meaningful way with that friend, neighbor, co-worker, second cousin, or even first-time acquaintance. Remember: The general election of 2024 will likely be decided by a few thousand voters in a half dozen swing states. Your determination to be informed about what has gone down over the past four years and your willingness to lobby the undecided voter *could* decide whether America continues its downward trajectory or reverses course. Not that I want to put undue pressure on you…

So what exactly *are* those failed policies and missteps, and how have they impacted our culture and country? Glad you asked.

CHAPTER 1

COVID

JOHNNY ONE NOTES

Follow the science.

—Joe Biden (countless times)

Remember the ever-popular dire warnings from the president and members of his administration (especially the public health community) during the Covid pandemic?

"No one is safe until everyone is safe";

"The only people dying are the unvaccinated";

"The pandemic of the unvaccinated";

"Facemasks are the most powerful tool we have";

"Don't do your own research"; and

"The forever war."

The "trust us" chorus was consistent, relentless, and uninterested in dissenting opinion (aka "conspiracy theories"). And, of course, it was a narrative buttressed by a media all in on blatant government censorship.

And then, in the blink of an eye, real science began to reveal itself. Social distancing disappeared. Mask mandates were eliminated and their efficacy questioned. Dr. Fauci retired. Rochelle Walensky announced her resignation from the Centers for Disease Control and Prevention. The Energy Department and Federal Bureau of Investigation finally admitted the Wuhan lab leak was the most likely origin of the pandemic. And Joe Biden said nothing. Similar to the aftermath of the Russia hoax, the Hunter Biden/fifty-one national security experts hoax, and the "country is being overrun by white supremacists" hoax, the people who run the place—and the people who report on the people who run the place—fell silent. There would be no mea culpas, no "Maybe we should have welcomed more constructive criticism" retrospectives, no "What have we done to our schoolchildren?" remorse. Only a narcissistic conviction of no regrets—"We did great things!"—as amplified by a compliant (and implicated) media.

THE BOTTOM LINE: And Washington wonders why flyover America has such disdain for the swamp.

THE U.S. MILITARY

*Our men and women in uniform should
never have been stripped of the benefits
they earned in the first place.*

—U.S. Rep. Scott Fitzgerald (R-WI) upon
introducing a bill that would ensure Honorable
Discharge status for soldiers who refused
the Covid vaccine, January 13, 2023

The all-volunteer armed forces have enjoyed a solid record of reaching recruitment goals. Indeed, those of us of a certain age have happy memories of the iconic "Be All That You Can Be" Army marketing campaign initiated during the Reagan era. The equal-parts message of self-challenge and patriotic duty was a no-brainer. But that was then…

Compare that happy messaging to the Biden administration's decision to terminate more than 8,000 active-duty service members for failure to meet the government's Covid-19 vaccine mandate. The timing of the mass firing could not have been worse. First there was the chaotic and deadly withdrawal from Afghanistan, with its attendant humiliation for the armed forces. Then came a campaign of woke messaging from a Pentagon focused more on progressive gender ideology than readiness. And all this during a time China was ramping up its own maximum-pressure campaign against Taiwan.

The off-ramping of active-duty troops in the cause of universal vaccination was poorly timed and sent the wrong message to the world's troublemakers. The fact that the policy was unsupported by the science only made a bad situation worse.

**THE BOTTOM LINE: Score another one for optics
over science, and politics over people.**

BIG TECH SUPPRESSION

It was not the public statements that were the problem. It was the alleged use of government agencies and employees to coerce and/or significantly encourage social media platforms to suppress free speech on those platforms.

—U.S. District Judge Terry Doughty
in *Missouri vs. Biden*, 2023

The introduction of Covid vaccines produced extraordinarily close coordination and cooperation between Biden administration executive branch agencies and social media platforms. Many of the communications concerned vax-related information the government wished to disparage pertaining to vaccine hesitancy, vaccine effectiveness, and the efficacy of alternative therapies and treatments.

Still, the fact that numerous of the CDC's opinions proved wildly inaccurate was not the genesis of a lawsuit brought by the attorneys general of Louisiana and Missouri. That litigation focused on the intensive coordination (including intimidation and strong-arm tactics) between government and social media giants on the issue of vaccine hesitancy—the degree of which the plaintiffs interpreted as a "sprawling federal Censorship Enterprise" that allowed Big Tech to remove unfavored (conservative) viewpoints. An injunction was accordingly issued by Trump-appointed judge Terry Doughty.

The usual suspects reacted with the usual outrage. To wit: Nina Jankowicz of Disinformation Governance Board fame feared the preliminary injunction "could unleash false information in critical areas of public life." The impacted White House staff and senior personnel operating in eleven different federal agencies weren't too happy either. And there will assuredly be additional appellate rounds to go on the issue.

THE BOTTOM LINE: In the short term at least, score one for free expression over Biden-era suppression.

SCHOOL CLOSURES

When schoolchildren start paying union
dues, that's when I'll start representing
the interests of schoolchildren.

—Albert Shanker, United
Federation of Teachers

The overwhelming circumstantial evidence is that Covid-19 sprang from a lab leak at the Wuhan Institute of Virology at some point in 2019. The death toll is estimated to be in excess of 6.9 million people. Untold millions more got sick and lost their jobs and businesses as governments brought economic activity to a crushing halt. But it will be many years before the total toll on our children can be quantified. Prolonged school shutdowns kept kids out of classrooms and away from hands-on learning. Zoom lessons picked up part of the learning shortfall, but there is unanimity of opinion that long-term school closings explain a precipitous decline in post-Covid standardized testing, as math scores plummeted to the lowest levels since 1990 and reading scores fell to their lowest levels since 2004.

Less obvious but real damage was inflicted by bell-curve-bending, social-promotion-friendly teachers and administrators who pushed marginal students through their academic requirements (let alone the damage incurred through woke-inspired "lessons" that came to light as parents watched them unfold on their kids' computer screens). Without doubt, college admissions officers (and future employers) will be forced to deal with this lurking skills problem when they see it.

Another sector of well-chronicled damage is mental health. Survey after survey reported dramatic increases in anxiety, depression and suicide among college age young adults. There is indeed a high price to pay for prolonged social isolation.

The foregoing damage was magnified by the determination of the Biden administration and teachers' unions to delay in-person learning for as long as possible, beyond the time scientists said it was safe to resume in-person school activities. More than a few pundits concluded that reliance on "the science" sure seemed more situational than it used to be.

THE BOTTOM LINE: Maybe you didn't hear it here first, but teachers' unions are far more about teachers than about students.

CHAPTER 2

CRIME

DEFUND THE POLICE

> *It's status quo thinking, and it's
> misinformed, to think that putting more
> cops on the street creates more safety.*
>
> —Vice Presidential candidate
> Kamala Harris, June 19, 2020

The post-George Floyd enthusiasm for defunding local police in deep-blue venues began to wane when violent crime waves spiked in those same cities. (Who would have thought murderers and rapists followed the daily news so closely?) Democrats of a lesser progressive bent led the way. Many of them represented districts where association with the defund movement meant big problems on election day.

President Biden repeatedly counted himself in this group. But facts on the ground raised questions: a January 2022 proposed executive order sought to limit local police access to so-called "military assets" (vehicles and equipment) and impose stringent conditions on the ability of local police to access federal grants. Notably, the proposed order was issued at the same time police recruitment numbers were continuing to crumble around the country.

"Defund the police" by another name does not work. Too cute by half doesn't cut it when public safety is an issue. Congressional Republicans repeatedly made this point, but the executive order took effect May 25, 2023.

THE BOTTOM LINE: If a new idea sounds silly and unworkable…it probably is.

TWO-TIERED JUSTICE

Show me the man and I'll show you the crime.

—Lavrentiy Beria, Stalin's secret police chief

Numerous books have been devoted to Hillary Clinton's questionable actions vis-à-vis her unsecured server, her 30,000 deleted emails, and her (admitted) act of wiping clean her server and destroying her communications devices. And yet then FBI Director James Comey opined to the Justice Department that "no reasonable prosecutor" would bring a case against her. More recently, President Biden has admitted to inappropriate stowing of confidential papers (from his days as vice president) at three different venues. His Justice Department will not be holding him responsible. And then there is the matter of Hunter Biden, who was ever so close to a notoriously sweetheart deal with friendly federal prosecutors…until a judge exposed the shenanigans and placed everyone in timeout (after which an indictment followed).

Now juxtapose the above with four indictments (two secured by Democratic prosecutors who *campaigned* on a "Get Trump" platform and two others brought by an uber Democratic "special counsel" whose specialty had been prosecution of war crimes) and you have—for at least half the country—what looks much like a two-tiered system of justice.

At some point the political parties in D.C. may get back to a rough equilibrium that distinguishes political witch hunts from criminal acts. As long as Donald J. Trump is part of the national political scene, however, that point in time is unlikely to be anytime soon.

Note the two Trump impeachments from his tenure as president are independent from this analysis, because impeachment is a political process unrelated to criminal indictments.

THE BOTTOM LINE: Establishments experiencing existential threats will do whatever they need to do to protect themselves.

CASHLESS BAIL

[Cash bail is a] modern day debtors' prison.

—Candidate Joe Biden circa the
2020 presidential campaign

Who among us believes poor people should be penalized for being poor? The answer: nobody. Nevertheless, criminal justice zealots are bringing the cashless bail initiative to a state near…you.

But, as usual, the facts on the ground are more nuanced. Most folks outside the criminal justice system do not know that judges are *mandated* to weigh the nature of the alleged crime, past criminal offenses, the personal resources of the accused, the risk of the accused not showing up for trial, and the risk to public safety when imposing cash bail. And then there is that good ol' Eighth Amendment that insures "excessive bail" not be imposed—a right that many state constitutions have expanded to the benefit of the accused. All this means that traditional bail is not an arbitrary remnant of the stone age that seeks to punish poor offenders on the basis of their (lack of) income.

Herein lies another example of how precarious the Biden-Harris approach to public safety is for the average citizen. Cashless bail for violent offenders makes for dangerous streets. Here, even those accused of *violent* crime can qualify for immediate bail. Those folks demanding "equity" within the criminal justice system may not have thought this through.

THE BOTTOM LINE: More innocents will pay a serious price as a result of cashless bail.

HUNTING AND ARCHERY PROGRAMS

This is shameful, but not at all surprising. The Biden administration will take any opportunity to stomp on your constitutional rights—even down to teaching kids archery and hunting skills.

—U.S. Rep. Dan Bishop (R-NC)
tweet, July 28, 2023

In June 2023, the Biden Department of Education announced that grant funding for shooting sports under the Elementary and Secondary Education Act (ESEA) would be eliminated.

The department claimed its decision was derived from the plain language of the Bipartisan Safer Communities Act—a bill passed in the aftermath of a string of horrific school shootings across the country. The language at issue stated that no federal funds would be spent on "training in the use of a dangerous weapon." The decision impacted well over a million students enrolled in archery and hunting education activities.

The decision roiled GOP members of Congress, sportsmen, and hunter education teachers who certify half a million students in the shooting arts annually. But few could argue they were surprised by a notoriously anti-gun administration intent on degrading a rural (read: red) American lifestyle.

THE BOTTOM LINE: The culture wars know no bounds…including your child's archery set.

CITIES

[Compared to 2019 mid-year figures, MCCA member] cities have experienced a 50 percent increase in homicides and a roughly 36 percent increase in aggravated assaults.

—Major Cities Chiefs Association
survey, September 2022

American cities are blue strongholds. Always have been, regardless of whether a white or black Democratic machine runs the place. But Biden-era policies—and George Soros-sponsored prosecutors—have taken some urban hubs to unheard-of lows.

Note that this is not simply a right-wing indictment. What not so long ago were relatively safe and beautiful cities

(Austin, San Francisco, Portland, Seattle) have been shattered by a deadly combination of progressive prosecutors, spiking violent crime, an explosion in homelessness, declining public schools, and a shrinking tax base.

This last element is most illustrative: The Biden era has witnessed dramatic taxpayer flight from blue cities unmatched since the social unrest of the 1960s. Nearly every week, some big-box chain—or small retail pharmacy—has announced they just couldn't take it anymore and were either going to shutter their doors and/or leave for safer environs. That these enterprises are escaping blue mostly coastal locales for the South or West, usually a red-state destination, is irony impossible to miss.

There are different iterations of a bumper sticker seen around Florida. It reads: "If you've come here from a blue place…leave your politics at the border." One can only hope.

THE BOTTOM LINE: Those who can least afford to leave invariably pay the heaviest price for progressive social experiments within America's most populus cities.

INTENDED CHAOS

Under this administration every state is now a border state. Every state is being forced to deal with the consequences of a border that is becoming little more than a line on a map.

—Rep. Juan Ciscomani (R-AZ) in
testimony before the House Committee on
Homeland Security, December 7, 2023

"Gang Jumps and Beats Two New
York City Police Officers."

"College Jogger Murdered in Georgia."

"Violent Assault on Border Agent in Texas."

"Illegal Immigrant Charged with Murder of
Toddler after Multiple Prior Arrests."

"Illegal Immigrant Arrested in NYC
for Beating Man with Rock."

"Deadly Venezuelan Gang Setting Up
in the U.S., Officials Warn."

"Illegal Migrant Murder Suspect
Rearrested in Rhode Island."

"Venezuela Releasing Prisoners into the United States."

"Riot Erupts after Migrant Swarm Steamrolls
U.S. National Guard Troops."

"More Chinese Illegal Migrants Apprehended at
Southern Border in Two Days than in all of 2021."

A sampling of storylines and headlines (I could go on for many more pages) from around the country as Joe Biden's porous border brought violent consequences to the American heartland.

These and so many similar crimes were committed by illegal migrants who had no right to be here in the first place. Even worse, some were the result of officials in sanctuary jurisdictions deciding to ignore ICE detainers even for violent repeat offenders. Now is a good time to remember that this is the way sanctuary cities are intended to operate.

THE BOTTOM LINE: American citizens have paid a steep price indeed for Mr. Biden's lawless border—a price progressive journalists and politicians dismissed as right-wing conspiracy theory for the better part of the last four years. Only a national election can fix what is so utterly broken.

CHAPTER 3

ECONOMY

INTEREST RATES

I don't know what the hell that is.

—President Joe Biden on
Bidenomics, June 17, 2023

*Thanks to Bidenomics, we're
restoring the American dream.*

—President Joe Biden tweet, August 10, 2023

Biden-era economic turmoil is not a complicated story. Unbridled, gratuitous spending during the final months of the Covid pandemic sparked a dramatic uptick in inflation, which in turn caused the Federal Reserve to raise interest rates. Here, Fed Chairman Jerome Powell made it clear that consistently rising rates will be the Fed's inflation-killing calling card for the intermediate future.

Higher interest rates mean higher debt service for job creators and make it more expensive to refinance existing debt.

Sound planning and growth are twin casualties. Bankruptcy filings in 2023 accordingly reached levels not seen since the recession of 2010.

The doubling or even tripling of the cost of capital after years of historically low interest rates and easy credit is the real culprit behind the Biden-era cycle of distress across all economic sectors. Even a more incremental approach to rate hikes is unlikely to bring much relief. Only a serious long-term plan to chill the federal spending spigot will help. Unfortunately, the left's (and Biden's) enthusiasm for unbridled federal spending—as reflected in the 2023 debt limit negotiations—offers no grounds for optimism.

THE BOTTOM LINE: There is no progressive appetite for even a modicum of fiscal restraint…just more of the same as federal debt accelerates past $34 trillion. The Biden era's higher interest rates will continue to make daily living an even more expensive proposition for the average American.

DEBT AND THE DEBT CEILING

Ultimately, this is more than just numbers on a balance sheet…. We owe it to ourselves and future generations to get our fiscal house in order and put our country on a path to long-term prosperity.

—U.S. Sen. Mike Lee (R-UT), Fox News op-ed, May 17, 2023

Democrats seem to win *every* intramural budget showdown over continuing resolutions and debt limit increases. The reason is simple: spending constituencies hold a dominant position within the Democratic Party and enthusiasm for ever-increasing expenditures is shared by the usual suspects within the mainstream media. And—truth be told—a similar if less dominant spending preference exists in more moderate GOP precincts as well.

This familiar scenario played out again in the debt ceiling showdown of 2023, albeit with a few twists. Here, Speaker Kevin McCarthy's slim four-vote margin necessitated early entreaties to the executive branch—entreaties which were summarily rejected ("I will not negotiate" was the president's stated position from the jump) until the very eve of the deadline.

It was at that point that President Biden blinked (sorta) with a few concessions regarding discretionary spending and a strengthened welfare work requirement—but no entitlement reform of any kind. Accordingly, the prime accelerant behind America's ticking time bomb of debt went unaddressed—again—while the country accumulated a deficit of $1.62 trillion for the first ten months of the fiscal year…and America's debt tin can continued its bumpy journey down the proverbial road.

THE BOTTOM LINE: Neither party is serious about balancing the federal budget. Republicans (at times) talk the talk, but Democrats don't even bother to pretend anymore.

INFLATION

*I think I was wrong then about the path that
inflation would take.... There have been
unanticipated and large shocks that have
boosted energy and food prices, and supply
bottlenecks that affected our economy badly, that
I didn't—at the time—didn't fully understand."*

—Treasury Secretary Janet Yellen to
CNN's Wolf Blitzer, June 1, 2022

Recall the basic facts: A Wuhan lab leak (the likely takeaway) sparks a pandemic. Economic activity diminishes overnight as businesses are forced to close down. The feds go on a money-printing binge despite being $30 trillion in debt—and then print more money in the waning days of Covid-19. The predictable result: Inflationary pressures go on a tear (despite the Treasury secretary's promise the inflationary spike would be "temporary"). Gas goes to five dollars a gallon and eggs to ten dollars a dozen and home heating oil through the roof. Twenty-six months of collapsing real wages followed. Fact: Median U.S. household income fell 2.3 percent in 2022 (the third year in a row under Joe Biden), but inflation rose 7.8 percent. Another fact: In October 2023, the Bureau of Labor Statistics reported prices spiked 3.7 percent over the previous twelve months, but core inflation was even higher at 4.1 percent. The cost of shelter—including rent and hotels—shot up 7.2 percent.

Basic economics teaches that inflation is the result of too many dollars chasing too few goods. Here, too many newly printed dollars chased too few goods while *production was still shuttered*—which meant *a lot* more dollars began chasing *far* fewer goods. A recovering economy took the brunt of the resulting hurt. And as usual, it was the poor and working poor that bore the disproportionate burden of bad fiscal policy.

THE BOTTOM LINE: Inflation is the meanest tax of all as the people who can least afford it (the poor) suffer disproportionate harm.

CREDIT RATING DOWNGRADE

Our base case expectation is that Fitch will be pilloried by most members of Congress.

—Henrietta Treyz, Director of Macro Economic Policy Research at Beda Partners, as quoted in the *New York Times*, August 1, 2023

In the dog days of August 2023, headlines blared the bad news: Fitch Ratings had downgraded America's credit ranking for the second time in U.S. history. This was big news in the financial markets. Still, the country yawned.

Fitch attributed the downgrade to deteriorating Washington credibility on fiscal policy. In other words, a major rating agency had seen the political establishment's lack of intestinal fortitude on a long-term budget fix and acted accordingly. Fitch added that recent debt ceiling negotiations provided only "modest improvement to the medium-term fiscal outlook."

Relatively few Americans understood that interest rates on consumer goods would soon reflect the move. But consumers weren't the only losers here. Biden's post-Covid spending binge took another hit. The public was reminded how Republicans had oversold their "win" at the recent debt ceiling showdown. And Uncle Sam (via another hit to the dollar) suffered a setback at a time China had gone all in on its campaign to replace the dollar as the world's reserve currency.

THE BOTTOM LINE: My favorite one-liner while a member of Congress: Republicans are the party of big government while Democrats are the party of *really* big government. Things haven't changed much in twenty years.

WAGE DISCRIMINATION

Women—working full-time, year-round—are paid 84 cents for every dollar paid to men. Those disparities are more pronounced for women of color and women with disabilities. On Equal Pay Day, we call attention to an injustice that undermines women's economic security.

—Joe Biden tweet, March 14, 2023

Progressive virtue signaling is bad. Virtue signaling while living in a glass house is worse. But virtue signaling while disconnected from reality is rock bottom.

Think of the above-captioned tweet wherein the Biden White House bemoans racism and sexism as the primary culprits of wage discrimination. The moral high ground is thereby captured. Yep, those dirty purveyors of wage discrimination are officially in the Biden administration's crosshairs.

Alas, the tweet was met with widespread derision (including an excellent takedown by Joe Perry of the American Enterprise Institute) when it was reported that women made 20 percent less money than men…at the Biden White House.

But here comes the disconnected part. This fact by itself does not mean Joe Biden discriminates against women. Real-world wage analysis is only achieved when apples are measured against apples—not oranges. In this case, any fair wage comparison must include factors such as years of experience, actual hours worked, educational attainment, relative dangers involved, and special talents. You know, apples to apples.

THE BOTTOM LINE: It's a tough league when even Joe Biden can't get his virtue signaling straight.

FARMING OUT

Making America more like Europe gives the Biden administration the government it wants, but European economic results won't give American families what they want.

—Phil Gramm and Jeb Hensarling, *Wall Street Journal* op-ed, October 18, 2023

President Joe Biden is most comfortable doing what he has done his entire political career: raise taxes. But the 2022 midterms turned the House red, which was a death knell for tax increases of all iterations.

Still, the specter of all those greedy entrepreneurs making *big* money but escaping "their fair share" of taxation grated on the progressive president. Most upsetting was the absence of a minimum corporate tariff. What to do?

Well…why not strike a deal to allow foreign governments to tax U.S. companies on their domestic (U.S.) profits (or the profits of subsidiaries doing business in their countries) so long as Congress refuses to adopt a minimum corporate tax regime as sponsored by the Organization for Economic Cooperation and Development. In other words, farm out one of your favorite tax schemes to a nongovernmental foreign actor that will do the dirty work for you.

Alas, former Senate Banking Committee Chairman Phil Gramm and former House Financial Services Chairman Jeb Hensarling exposed the leverage play on the op-ed page of the *Wall Street Journal*. Score another W on behalf of a free press.

THE BOTTOM LINE: The last thing American business owners need is for the federal government to emulate the anti-growth tax regimes of Western Europe.

JUNK FEES

Many people want the government to protect the consumer. A much more urgent problem is to protect the consumer from the government.

—Milton Friedman, American economist

It sounds so good when you say it real fast: "Cap credit card late fees." After all, who likes those huge, credit-card-issuing Wall Street banking monsters? Just a bunch of money-hungry capitalists if you ask Elizabeth Warren…and Joe Biden. (Yes, *that* Joe Biden, the former protector of the Delaware-based credit-card-issuing big banks.)

So, Mr. Biden's Consumer Financial Protection Bureau (CFPB) proposed a rule to cap late fees that can prove punishing for those living on the economic precipice. Here was a populist-themed move that seemed ripe for a class warfare television ad campaign against the profit-hungry banks.

But a variety of free market economists, including former Trump associate director for economic policy Vance Ginn, articulated the other side of the issue, pointing out that late fees provide incentive for people to live within their means, and the big banks would simply cover their losses by raising fees or increasing lending standards to make up for lost revenue (both moves having a detrimental impact on the poor and working poor). Not an illogical line of reasoning, but likely too deep for those simply looking for a cheap applause line.

THE BOTTOM LINE: Misguided policies can be well intended but nevertheless harmful to the intended beneficiaries.

TRICKLE DOWN

*Folks, let me say this as clearly as I can:
the trickle-down approach failed the
middle class. It failed America….*

—President Biden's remarks on
Bidenomics, June 28, 2023

Recent economic policy reveals that despite the left's repeated denials, federal tax cuts generate more—not less—revenue for the federal treasury. Such is the primary takeaway from the Kennedy, Reagan, Bush, and Trump tax cuts.

But this lesson in free market economics is more contested than it should be because the spending culture in Washington could not leave well enough alone. To wit: in the aftermath of major tax cuts, the bipartisan big spenders on Capitol Hill continue to spend far in excess of the additional revenue tax cuts generate—most recently, to the tune of a $35 trillion federal deficit (and counting).

The unfortunate result is that Democratic administrations continue to insist that tax cuts don't work—that they cost money, and only the wealthy benefit.

Joe Biden's pre-election budget (for fiscal year 2025) accordingly hit all the wrong class warfare notes: $5 trillion in new taxes *and* the expiration of the highly successful Trump tax cuts after 2025, what amounts to another $2 trillion in tax increases.

THE BOTTOM LINE: In November 2024, voters will make a binary decision: either a growth-killing tax increase or the continuation of the wildly successful Trump-era tax cuts.

BLAME GAME

"Corporate greed" and "price gouging" are driving higher prices and inflation.

—President Joe Biden (countless times)

Of course you're going to have inflation when Congress and the president are signing trillions of dollars of new spending and, again, pushing

*up annual deficits to $2 trillion a year. This
is textbook expansionary fiscal policy.*

—Brian Riedl, Senior Fellow,
Manhattan Institute

Per the Biden Treasury Department, America's national debt (defined as the amount of money the federal government borrows to cover ongoing operating expenses) is approaching $35 trillion and rising at a clip of approximately $1 trillion every hundred days. That math comes out to $8.5 billion dollars every day. But the math hardly causes a ripple in the nation's political dialogue.

The twin themes of class warfare and demonization of business are the never-changing "page one" of the left's playbook…because they work.

THE BOTTOM LINE: So dangerous but so familiar is the latest Biden gambit of blaming billionaires, corporate greed, and price gouging for the most recent round of spiking inflation. Fortunately, the envy-tinged narrative is lately getting lost in translation, mostly due to the incoherence of Biden's fiscal policies and the ever-increasing cost of living.

TAXING (NON)EVENTS

*[Biden's proposed tax on unrealized income]
will create new complexity in the tax code
and expand the power of the IRS. It will
wreak havoc on the economy and likely grow
to hit far more Americans than intended.*

—Isabelle Morales, Policy Communications
Specialist, Americans for Tax Reform

Joe Biden's tax-and-spend assault on American capitalism began a new chapter with a 2025 budget proposal calling for a 44.6 percent capital gains tax rate (on those with taxable income over $1 million and investment income exceeding $400,000). If passed and signed into law, the move would constitute the highest capital gains rate since 1922.

Herein another example of Washington, D.C.'s never-ending ways and means aimed at emptying taxpayers' pockets. Still, this most recent effort to raise rates is more likely a shot across the bow in order to first remind the ever-fleeing middle class that the evil "rich" *still* do not pay their fair share, and second, to lay a predicate for the left's shiny new scheme to tax unrealized appreciation of capital gains until such time as progressives have enough votes to actually pass it.

THE BOTTOM LINE: As my old seatmate and friend Congressman Sonny Bono used to say… "and the beat goes on." But how unfortunate that Biden's beat is always directed at higher taxes and ever more revenue for the federal coffers.

JIMMY CARTER REDUX

I look at the amount of fiscal and monetary stimulus that has taken place over the last five years—it has been so extraordinary, how can you tell me it won't lead to stagflation?

—Jamie Dimon, Chase CEO,
May 29, 2024

A decades-old economic malady made a sudden reappearance just as the weather turned warm in the late spring of 2024. Yes, the return of stagflation meant that Bidenomics had generated a cycle of sustained inflation *and* slow growth—a reality guaranteed to shake already middling consumer confidence just as the 2024 campaign began to heat up. It was a state of affairs eerily familiar to American consumers of a certain (Jimmy Carter era) age—an era that did not end well for the thirty-ninth president.

The GDP number for the first quarter of 2024 (1.6 percent) was indeed daunting: the economy grew at a pace less than half of the previous quarter and much slower than economists had predicted, while core consumer prices (absent food and energy) spiked by 3.8 percent.

THE BOTTOM LINE: The average worker felt what the Biden administration's fiscal leadership (and their apologists in the media) had been denying for months: real wages have declined under the Biden administration.

CHAPTER 4

EDUCATION

SCHOOL LOANS

> *People think that the president of the United*
> *States has the power for debt forgiveness.*
> *He does not. He can postpone. He can*
> *delay. But he does not have that power.*
> *That has to be an act of Congress.*
>
> —Speaker Nancy Pelosi on student
> debt forgiveness, July 28, 2021

A suddenly shut-down, pandemic-impacted economy prompted the Biden administration to seek a series of short-term "pauses" in student debt repayment. But pauses were not enough for Mr. Biden. In October 2022 the president introduced a plan to outright cancel up to $10,000 of debt per student (PELL grantees could receive up to $20,000 in relief)—a scheme that was itself placed on hold while the Supreme Court considered the constitutionality of executive debt forgiveness under the federal student loan program.

On June 30, 2023, the court struck down Mr. Biden's misuse of executive authority, citing the above quote. Two weeks later, Mr. Biden announced the "automatic discharge" of school debt on behalf of 804,000-plus federal loan borrowers who had earned forgiveness under income-driven repayment plans but due to "administrative failure" and "inaccurate payment counts" had failed to receive relief.

Note: I was a working-class kid who took out a school loan in order to attend Princeton, so I am sympathetic to the pressures that accompany significant post-college debt. What I never did understand was a proposal that would immediately cancel $10,000 in loans for those making up to $125,000 a year (which the Biden plan sought to accomplish) and disproportionately benefit those holding graduate degrees. Besides the specter of high school graduates paying off the debt of wealthier college types—and the equally disquieting smack in the face to the millions of graduates who have previously paid off their debt—there were other consequences, such as feeding tuition escalation and the subsidizing of low-value (unmarketable) degree programs. Simply put, the political football better known as "Biden loan relief" was a poorly thought-out remedy for a real-world problem.

THE BOTTOM LINE: Politically motivated giveaways may be popular but send the wrong message to the wider culture.

WOMEN'S SPORTS

Yikes!

—Tennis Star Martina Navratilova
when told soccer star Megan Rapinoe

would accept a transgender woman
replacing a biological female on the
U.S. women's national soccer team

By any measure, Title IX has been a smashing success for female athletes. New funding has led to more scholarships and more varsity teams at all levels of college athletics. Public interest has grown accordingly as TV-friendly sports such as women's basketball and lacrosse have generated the type of publicity and public attention that had once been reserved for men's sports.

But storm clouds gathered as the country commemorated the fiftieth anniversary of the groundbreaking law. Those storm clouds surrounded the appropriateness of biological men competing on female college athletic teams—an issue that came to a head with the awarding of an NCAA women's swimming championship to the University of Pennsylvania's Lia Thomas, a trans athlete who in prior years had competed on Penn's men's swimming team.

A woke NCAA, Ivy League, and Biden administration pretended there was nothing unique about an outcome wherein a physically imposing Thomas smashed female competitors despite previous limited success on the men's team. The crisis grew as other biological men began to participate in—and dominate—other women's sports, especially track.

Civil rights activists were conflicted. The woke elements celebrated the accomplishments of the trans athletes, but a growing constituency (led by University of Kentucky swimmer Riley Gaines) took to the media bully pulpit to condemn the unfairness of it all—a position shared by the most famous trans athlete of them all: Caitlin Jenner.

Red America could not help but see the irony of (some) feminists celebrating the maturation of women's sports…while celebrating an existential threat to women's sports.

Footnote: On April 6, 2023, the Biden administration issued a proposed rule that would prevent an educational institution that is a recipient of federal dollars from banning trans individuals' participation in collegiate athletic events. This means that athletes would be welcome to play—and use the locker room facilities—of their chosen gender identity.

THE BOTTOM LINE: Gender-bending has crossed the line in women's sports—and young women athletes will continue to pay an awful price for it.

WOMEN'S SPORTS II: "I AM WOMAN"

I am woman, hear me roar
In numbers too big to ignore

—Helen Reddy, "I Am Woman," 1973

The above was a major hit for Canadian singer Helen Reddy. It also morphed into a type of feminist anthem during the women's rights movement of the 1970s.

That catchy tune came to mind on April 19, 2024, when Joe Biden announced that gender would replace biological sex under Title IV of the Civil Rights Act, meaning that "gender identity" would become a new protected class under federal civil rights law. In effect, with a stroke of the pen, Joe Biden decreed that biological sex and gender identity would henceforth no longer be differentiated under federal law.

This dramatic move means that biological men are now eligible for female athletic scholarships, can compete against biological women in athletic contests, and are able to access female bathrooms and locker rooms. To boot, students, family, and administrators are required to utilize the preferred pronouns of trans athletes or face harassment charges.

Note that this stunning move will assuredly lead to further confusion in women's intercollegiate athletics and extend litigation well beyond the November election—actions that will be rendered moot should Mr. Trump once again assume the presidency.

THE BOTTOM LINE: As the second stanza of "I Am Woman" reads, "Yes, I've paid the price, but look how much I've gained." Words that now ring hollow following Joe Biden's assault on biology.

DUE PROCESS

If a college student is to be marked for life as a sexual predator, it is reasonable to require that he be provided a fair opportunity to defend himself, and an impartial arbiter to make that decision.

—U.S. District Judge Dennis F. Saylor IV
in *Doe vs. Brandeis University*, 2016

Most Americans associate Title IX with female athletics, and for good reason. The groundbreaking law has dramatically raised the profile (and popularity) of women's sports.

But there is another application of sex-based discrimination that is less well known—the due process that is supposed to provide protections to both complainants and respondents in alleged sexual assault cases on campus. All of which begs a central question: Exactly which due process rules are operational in order to ensure the most equitable treatment of both parties in these often emotional "he said/she said" cases? Unfortunately, the answer seems to depend on which political party is in power.

You see, the Department of Education issues the rules applicable in Title IX hearings. And—you guessed it—a brand-new Biden DOE issued revised rules, effectively undoing a number of due process protections previously implemented by Trump DOE Secretary Betsy DeVos.

Per these new rules, *one person* can act as investigator, judge, and sentencer; a lesser standard of "preponderance of evidence" (as opposed to a higher "clear and convincing standard") is enough to "convict" a respondent; the definition of sexual harassment is broadened sufficiently enough to include *speech* that is subjectively offensive; the right to in-person cross-examination is effectively eliminated; and accused students are no longer provided the right to review all the evidence against them—only a "description of the relevant evidence." Yikes!

THE BOTTOM LINE: Obama-era due process limitations are back in vogue. Accused students are again in the crosshairs, and fair treatment is again in jeopardy on American campuses.

NATIONAL ARCHIVES

> *The Catalog and web pages [of the National Archives] contain some content that may be harmful or difficult to view.... As a result, some of the materials presented here may reflect outdated, biased, offensive, and possibly violent views and opinions.*
>
> —National Archives and Records Administration online statement on potentially harmful content

Progressives never miss an opportunity to indict American history. The attraction is particularly strong when the object of the scorn is a "racist" founding father. And so, the Biden-era National Archives decided it appropriate to add a "harmful language alert" to the country's foundational documents.

Yes, you read that correctly. The wokesters we pay to gather, protect, and display America's most important historical artifacts to a world audience thought it appropriate to add trigger warnings to displays of the Declaration of Independence, the Constitution, and the Bill of Rights.

What not so long ago would have been satire is now woke reality.

THE BOTTOM LINE: If you have ever wondered whether future generations will look back on our progressive era with a combination of amusement and disgust, you can now stop wondering.

CHARTER SCHOOLS

*I'm challenging these backwards Biden
administration rules and fighting
alongside parents to secure and expand
opportunity for all children.*

—U.S. Sen. Tim Scott (R-SC),
September 9, 2022

In the summer of 2022, the Biden Department of Education issued new rules that increased obstacles for schools attempting to qualify for federally sponsored charter grants. An amended application process would require aspiring applicants to prove the local public school was over-enrolled (not simply failing to educate its students) in order to secure the federal grant.

Bipartisan criticism of the "one-size-fits-all" reforms ensued, but the Biden administration did not back down. Of course, ever more obstacles on the road to school autonomy is the goal for those who view the charter movement as an existential threat to the education establishment. You see, despite relentless opposition from teachers' unions and elected Democrats, charters have proven to be successful—and wildly popular—especially in economically challenged neighborhoods and among minority parents.

THE BOTTOM LINE: A movement that began in Minnesota in 1991 and was championed by African American legislators in Wisconsin and other states by the mid-1990s has blossomed into a school choice revolution—and a serious challenge to union power in the American classroom.

CURRICULUM

*I don't think parents should be telling
schools what they should teach.*

—Virginia Gov. Terry McAuliffe during a
gubernatorial debate, September 29, 2021

Loudoun County, Virginia may have been the epicenter of the
parental rights movement, but much of what drove the parents' narrative concerned events that took place outside the
classroom: sexual assaults, administrative cover-ups, bad-faith
maneuverings by the Justice Department, and an upset GOP
win in what had become a reliably blue state.

Central to the story was the issue of curriculum. Specifically,
the willingness of progressive educators and school boards to
exchange "three-R learning" for woke revisionist instruction
while lowering performance thresholds on standardized tests.
The resulting controversies extended far beyond whether 1776
or 1619 represents the core founding of America. Here, the
issue often revolved more around the enthusiasm of (some)
administrators and teachers for explicit sex instruction and
inappropriate literature in *elementary and middle schools* without parental permission.

**THE BOTTOM LINE: I do not know when the long-
established line of "hands off kids" was crossed,
but here we are with a national administration
seemingly okay with this dangerous new frontier.**

LOUDOUN COUNTY, VIRGINIA

[The FBI will take the lead in investigating]
a disturbing spike in harassment,
intimidation, and threats of violence
against school administrators, board
members, teachers, and staff.

—Memo from U.S. Attorney General
Merrick Garland, October 5, 2021

The story begins with a report of a sexual assault against a teenage girl in a Loudoun County, Virginia, public school. A subsequent report offered additional facts: the assault was allegedly committed by a boy who had been transferred to that school after a previous sexual assault.

The facts took on additional complexity when the father of the victim was arrested at a "raucous school board meeting." (A video of the arrest and resulting chaos went viral.) And then a grand jury report revealed that administrators had failed to follow adequate transparency, discipline, and transfer protocols from the jump.

Could even more malign factors come together to make this story worse? Oh yes. You see, a "sexual assault cover-up" is not a helpful narrative for the woke left, especially when "radicalized parents disrupt school board meeting" is such an appealing alternative. And so the Biden Department of Justice assisted the National School Board Association to fashion a letter (to itself) asking for assistance in the investigation of those disruptive/dangerous parents—a scheme that was subsequently exposed and cast further doubt on the integrity of the attorney general and Department of Justice. Sit back and think about those facts for a long minute one night.

Still, the administration's reckless employment of the FBI and disregard for parental rights had one upside as businessman Glenn Youngkin rode the issue of parents' rights to victory over former Gov. Terry McAuliffe in the Virginia gubernatorial election of 2021.

THE BOTTOM LINE: Too Cute By Half got caught in the act. Yet another embarrassing episode for the Biden DOJ.

RELIGIOUS INSTITUTIONS

We need to fight this tyranny from federal government agencies not only to stand up for ourselves but to ensure this type of ideological government overreach and weaponization of federal agencies does not happen to others.

—Grand Canyon University
President Brian Mueller

The secular left's disdain for faith-based instruction in the classroom is well established. But the outrage increases tenfold when it comes to religiously based institutions of higher learning. Here, not even a quarter is given to those who refuse woke guidance in the education of persuadable young minds.

And so Christian colleges found themselves in the left's crosshairs during the Biden era. Case in point: Grand Canyon University (the country's largest Christian school) was fined $37 million by Mr. Biden's Department of Education for the alleged sin of misrepresenting the true cost of a doctoral degree and false advertising in its marketing program—despite the fact that similar claims against the school (in a civil lawsuit) were previously dismissed.

The frontal attack on the school (the largest fine ever imposed by the DOE) was criticized by a host of right-leaning commentators, including the *Wall Street Journal* and conservatives in Congress, but to no avail. And the progressive campaign against career colleges and Christian institutions just kept on chuggin' along.

THE BOTTOM LINE: "All of the above" must be on America's higher education menu—and it must be inclusive of private vocational and religious institutions.

STUDENT LOANS

Over 40 million people were promised cancellation, a number that dwarfs the 3.7 million who have received some "measure of relief."

—Astra Taylor, co-founder of Debt Collective (a union for debtors)

In February 2024, Mr. Biden once again ventured into the abyss of the student loan world by putting forth yet another large-scale student debt forgiveness plan. This time the underlying rationale was so-called economic hardship whereby those experiencing difficulty in maintaining their daily finances could secure relief.

The administration presented its new program as a pragmatic approach on behalf of those most likely to default on their payments over the next few years. In other words, the nanny state would again bail out college and graduate school debtors on the backs of high school graduates and the millions of degree holders who had previously discharged their debt.

Adding insult to injury, Biden apologists stated that no taxpayer dollars would be involved in the buyout—as if forgiveness of a government debt obligation amounted to a financial no-count.

THE BOTTOM LINE: Herein all you need to know about how the federal government has run up $35 trillion in debt with no end in sight.

CHAPTER 5

ENERGY AND ENVIRONMENT

KEYSTONE XL PIPELINE

*The president must turn to American-
made energy and jobs rather than dictators
and despots to fix the energy crisis he
created on his first day in office.*

—U.S. Sens. Jim Risch (R-ID) and Steve
Daines (R-MT), January 6, 2023

The Keystone Pipeline runs from Alberta, Canada, to refineries in Illinois and Texas. A proposed additional pipeline (Keystone XL) was planned to connect terminals in Alberta to Steele City, Nebraska, after picking up additional volume of light crude from the Williston Basin of Montana and North Dakota.

The proposed extension was first delayed by President Obama before the Trump administration restarted the permit process on an expedited basis. And then Joe Biden issued an executive order to revoke the permit—on his first day in office.

The proposed extension was projected to create 11,000 new high-paying construction jobs (in addition to an already-existing 1,500 jobs) in addition to increased domestic energy security during a time of post-pandemic growing demand.

Two years later, Biden's Department of Energy (fulfilling a mandate that the department provide a comprehensive analysis of the costs associated with the cancellation) projected the pipeline would have created between 16,000 and 59,000 jobs with an economic impact of between $3.16 billion and $9.16 billion.

THE BOTTOM LINE: That some energy field workers voted for Joe Biden—and against their economic self-interest— speaks to the (still) relevant power of organized labor.

STRATEGIC PETROLEUM RESERVE

Recently, Bloomberg Energy reporter Ari Natter pointed out that while it only took six months for the Biden administration to sell 180 million barrels from the SPR in the "fastest withdrawal on record," it will likely take decades to refill the SPR to capacity, "if it happens at all."

—Jeff Eshelman, President and CEO,
Independent Petroleum Association
of America, July 24, 2023

America's Strategic Petroleum Reserve (SPR) exists to minimize the impact of energy supply shortfalls. It has always been viewed as a last option in the face of a cataclysmic oil shortage.

Nevertheless, the Biden administration released over 200 million barrels from the Reserve prior to the 2022 midterms at a time escalating gas prices was a hot political issue. The decision lowered the SPR to its lowest level since 1984. The ploy also resulted in reduced short-term gas prices at the pump, precisely as intended. That a depleted SPR reflects the dependent nature of Biden-era energy policy, while leaving America vulnerable to market manipulation by often hostile producers, went unaddressed by the administration and the mainstream media.

In a related note: House Republicans made numerous requests for documents from Biden's Department of Energy regarding the release but were repeatedly stonewalled by Secretary Jennifer Granholm's staff. Alas, media coverage of the brazen move diminished as gas prices stabilized.

THE BOTTOM LINE: Manipulating the SPR for political purposes is bad precedent—and a bad moral—but it works.

OIL I

I think he has been wrong on nearly every major foreign policy and national security issue over the past four decades.

—Obama Defense Secretary Bob Gates on Joe Biden's foreign policy record, circa 2014

Once in power, the Biden administration wasted no time in implementing its priority environmental initiative: a "Green New Deal" (GND) regulatory approach in the energy sector.

The move ensured America's days as an energy-independent superpower would soon end. Mr. Biden then doubled down through a series of attacks on Saudi Arabia, an important strategic partner during the time the Trump administration pursued peace deals with other Sunni states while conducting a maximum-pressure campaign against Iran.

But when Vladimir Putin invaded Ukraine, the West (especially the U.S.) promised retaliation against Russian oil—a measure that proved worthless as the demand for Putin's oil in the West (and China) did not abate. As a consequence, a newly empowered Russian/Saudi axis sold oil (far above Trump-era prices), thereby helping to finance Russia's latest war of aggression and reestablishing the Saudis as cartel price-setters. Add in an inflationary spike caused by rising domestic energy prices and you have a Biden "four-fer":

1. A Green New Deal-friendly U.S. administration left to beg unfriendly but energy-rich despots and miscreants for their dirty energy;

2. A liquid Russia war machine;

3. A Saudi policy redirect into the waiting hands of Russia/China; and

4. An energy price shock in the U.S.

In May of 2023, the entity charged with domestic grid monitoring, the North American Electric Reliability Corporation, warned that two thirds of the country could experience power outages in the event of a hot summer.

THE BOTTOM LINE: Unilateral disarmament in energy production hurts American consumers while empowering the world's worst dictators. It makes no sense.

OIL II

*The only existential threat humanity faces
even more frightening than a nuclear
war is global warming going above 1.5
degrees in the next twenty to ten years.*

—President Joe Biden, September 11, 2023

The storyline narrative is oh so familiar by now: Hurricanes in the Caribbean? Climate change. Wildfires in Canada? Climate change. An especially hot August? Climate change. Brutal cold spell in February? Climate change. The University of Alabama football team goes 12 and 0? Climate change.

The Biden-Harris administration played into the narrative early and never took its foot off the accelerator. That the administration's regulatory initiatives reflected the ideology was not surprising. What was disquieting was the administration's willingness to proceed with untested (in some cases underperforming) methods of carbon mitigation (carbon capture and sequestration and hydrogen blending) via EPA rulemaking with the knowledge that such premature reliance could result on grid unreliability and rolling blackouts.

Laymen are left to wonder how much "science" has entered into the left's climate change shaming campaign, especially now that a number of leading climate scientists (Judith Curry, Gregory Wrightstone, Patrick Moore, Will Happer) have cast hard science-based doubt on various tenets of climate religion (unsurprisingly underreported by a resistant media).

Despite the popular moniker, "science deniers" are nothing of the sort. The vast majority buy hard science results. Most believe alternatives should be part of an "all of the above" energy mix, but not prematurely so. Most are more than a bit irritated by nonscientists/politicians who engage in over-the-top rhetoric about our energy future. That just about all climate activists are not fans of profit, growth, development, competitive markets, and oil is not lost on the huddled masses.

THE BOTTOM LINE: The next time you watch a liberal-arts-major politician predict a catastrophic weather event—just change the channel.

ESG

ESG is the devil.

—Elon Musk on Twitter, June 14, 2023

Mentioning ESG, the latest no-no.

—Wall Street Journal headline,
January 19, 2024

A cornerstone rule of asset management requires investment professionals to maximize client returns—to act solely in the economic interest of client-shareholders. The obligation is known as "fiduciary duty." Breaches of this long-established standard of care can lead to investor lawsuits.

But the investment universe has recently been turned upside down by the arrival of three seemingly innocuous letters: ESG (Environmental, Social, and Governance). The concept is deceptively brilliant: leverage publicly held companies to adopt progressive policy agendas (not attainable through the legislative process) through board activism, even where such investment strategy may not result in the highest return on investment.

Here, lefty influencers get public boards to literally buy into a wide array of "social justice" causes, including abortion on demand, trans rights, racial preferences, and anything that smacks of green energy. In these contexts, large energy companies are instructed to stop drilling for oil, stockbrokers are encouraged to violate their fiduciary duty to clients, and large insurance carriers are encouraged to underwrite policies on the basis of race. That the ESG movement is generating considerable angst within corporate America is reflected in the above quotes, but is not enough to dissuade ESG's true believers— including the sitting president of the United States.

THE BOTTOM LINE: The next time you're confused about why some successful, established public company has gone all in on a polarizing (woke) advertising strategy sure to turn off a large segment of customers—think ESG.

GAS STOVES

Any option is on the table. Products that can't be made safe can be banned.

—Richard Trumka, Commissioner, U.S. Product Safety Commission, January 11, 2023

Consumer Product Safety Commissioner Richard Trumka's widely reported comment to the effect that his powerful agency was coming for America's gas stoves set off a firestorm of criticism. Various lefty pundits (per their usual modus operandi) alleged overreaction on the right—after which it was revealed that the gas stove initiative was but one front in a far larger effort targeting household appliances in the cause of Biden's Green New Deal regulatory offensive. Not one American can feign surprise at the timing of these announcements; the foregoing approach is by now quite familiar:

1. Break new ground with a distressingly progressive proposal sure to strike up angst in flyover America;

2. Utilize friendly media outlets to dismiss criticism as typical right wing conspiracy theory overreaction; and then

3. Quietly implement the controversial policy while public attention is diverted by other equally outrageous initiatives as reported by the 24/7 news cycle.

THE BOTTOM LINE: You have to give the devil his due. While a compliant media is indeed helpful, this passive-aggressive 3-D communications strategy ("Deny, Dismiss, Divert") has proven to be wildly effective.

EAST PALESTINE, OHIO

I'm taking some personal time.

—Transportation Secretary Pete Buttigieg
in response to the East Palestine train
derailment, February 21, 2023

On February 3, 2023, a Norfolk Southern freight train loaded with hazardous chemicals derailed in East Palestine, Ohio. Poisonous fires burned for two days, including a controlled burn that resulted in the release of hydrogen chloride and phosgene into the environment. Residents in the immediate vicinity of the crash site were evacuated as state and federal agencies took charge of the scene.

The spill killed thousands of fish and other marine animals in local streams, while local residents and emergency responders of the CDC experienced a variety of negative health reactions. The incident produced the usual litany of associated controversies, including the specter of aging railroad infrastructure, the effectiveness of federal railroad safety regulations, and adverse environmental consequences such as contaminated ground water.

But it was the lackluster response of Transportation Secretary Pete Buttigieg and the president himself that was most telling. East Palestine is predominately white, decidedly working class, and economically beaten down. In other words, Donald Trump country. (Trump carried the town by a margin of more than two to one over Joe Biden in 2020.) In that context, its plight did not comport with any progressive "victim" narrative. It was accordingly unsurprising the president would leave the country (to visit Ukraine) in the midst of the crisis. Equally unsurprising was a quick and perfunctory Buttigieg visit that did not play to positive reviews. A Trump visit on February 22 (complete with thousands of bottles of Trump drinking water) *was* well received by East Palestine's beleaguered residents.

Epilogue: On September 2, 2023, the president remarked that although he wanted to make a visit to East Palestine, he was simply "too busy" to make it happen. This from the man who had spent much of the summer on vacation. Again, message received in flyover America.

THE BOTTOM LINE: Alas, empathy and, yes, symbolism still count when it comes to face time in the aftermath of God- and man-made disasters.

JOHN KERRY

When you have bombs going off and you have damage to septic tanks or to power centers, et cetera, you have enormous release of greenhouse gas of methane, all of the family of greenhouse gases, and the result is, it's adding to the problem.

—John Kerry on the "real" problem with
the war in Ukraine, July 10, 2023

John Kerry was a reliably hard-left vote during his years as a United States senator from Massachusetts. His message did not change during an unsuccessful run for president against George W. Bush in 2004 and a four-year stint as secretary of state under Barack Obama. But his climate alarmism and over-the-top green rhetoric *has* intensified during his tenure as Joe Biden's first-ever U.S. Special Presidential Envoy for Climate.

In this vein, the hits just keep on comin'. There was the 2009 assertion that unnamed scientists believed the Arctic would be "ice-free" by the summer of 2013. And the continuing lectures concerning the dangers inherent in economic growth. And his unapologetic defense of "climate leaders" who use private jets to attend…climate conferences. (Kerry himself flew on a private jet to Iceland in order to receive an *environmental award.*) And his incriminating admission that it would not matter if the U.S. and China were somehow able to achieve zero (carbon) emissions "tomorrow." And my personal favorite: comparing the sacrifice required to defeat Naziism to what it will take to defeat climate change—on the seventy-ninth anniversary of Pearl Harbor!

Throw in Kerry's contribution to the revitalization of the Iranian missile and nuclear development programs, and his dismissal of the Chinese Communist Party's grotesque record on human rights ("not my lane"), and you have the classic patrician progressive ready, willing, and able to sacrifice the working man's American dream in the interest of…maintaining credibility at Davos.

In January of 2024, with polls showing Biden's reelection effort trailing President Trump in a number of key states (and, notably, losing support of voters under thirty), Kerry left the administration in order to supercharge (and propagate) his climate alarmist message along the campaign trail.

THE BOTTOM LINE: A reminder about too close for comfort: John Kerry garnered 59,028,444 votes in the general election of 2004, only three million less than George W. Bush.

JOHN KERRY II (RIDICULOUSNESS)

*[John Kerry's words were] Sick. Dangerous.
And totally immoral to suggest you can
conduct wars of aggression in Europe so
long as you support the green agenda.*

—Mike Pompeo, Former U.S. Secretary of State

On his way out the door as climate envoy, Mr. Kerry again landed in Outrageous World when he suggested that the free world might "feel better" toward Vladimir Putin's horrific war of aggression in Ukraine if the totalitarian power would commit to reducing its carbon emissions.

The truly ludicrous statement drew plenty of criticism, outrage, and bewilderment from those living on planet Earth (witness the above-cited quote from the former secretary of state).

Making matters worse was the timing of the statement, as Ukraine's much-anticipated 2023 summer/fall counteroffensive had ground down to a high-casualty war of attrition in the face of superior Russian troop strength and armaments.

THE BOTTOM LINE: Numerous commentators on the right use the term "disconnected" to describe Mr. Kerry's tin-ear, out-of-touch comments. I am at a loss to come up with a better adjective.

PARIS

*In 2020, China brought 38.4 gigawatts of new
coal-fired plants into operation, more than three
times what was brought online everywhere else.*

—*Yale Environment 360*, March 24, 2021

The Paris Climate Accords were adopted by 196 countries in 2015. The agreement covered climate mitigation and finance, with the agreed-upon goal of (carbon) admissions reduction to net zero by the mid-twenty-first century. Of special note is the obligation of each participant to submit an action plan every five years, despite the absence of any enforcement mechanism.

The back-and-forth of American participation is familiar. The U.S. originally joined during the Obama administration. President Trump—fulfilling a campaign promise—began a departure process that commenced in 2017 and was completed in 2020. President Biden—also fulfilling a campaign promise—brought America back on board in 2021.

[Inconvenient] truth be told, the West (where carbon emissions continue to decrease) is not the issue. That moniker belongs to China, an original signatory in 2015 that has taken maximum advantage of the agreement's flexibility by implementing scheduled emissions increases until 2030. (Per the Centre for Research on Energy and Clean Air, China opened six times as many new coal-fired plants in 2022 than the rest of the world combined.) Does anyone seriously expect the ultra-nationalist, saber-rattling Xi Jinping to unilaterally curtail his domestic energy supply in a handful of years?

THE BOTTOM LINE: America's record on carbon reduction—especially during the Trump era—is an inconvenient fact seldom referenced by Western climate warriors.

STAR WARS AND SUN RAYS

*White House is pushing ahead research to
cool Earth by reflecting back sunlight.*

—CNBC Report, October 13, 2022

My initial reaction was to simply gloss over this bulletin. My second was to suspect I had happened upon a right-wing humor page—perhaps The Babylon Bee. And then I realized this story was not bogus, but rather another page out of the Biden administration's daily end-of-time climate change playbook.

One of the "key points" from CNBC's coverage: "Stratospheric aerosol injection [one of the sunlight reflection technologies under consideration] involves spraying an aerosol-like sulfur dioxide into the stratosphere, *and because it has the potential to affect the entire globe, often gets the most attention* [emphasis added]."

The truly amusing point was that, after digesting the news, I found myself back at my second thought: This can't be real. I mean, what could possibly go wrong with the climate religionists of the Biden era attempting to manipulate ("bioengineer") the sun's rays in order to escape the imminent death spiral of global warming?

THE BOTTOM LINE: I doubt whether the White House Office of Science and Technology would find any humor in my takeaway. But the fact that so many would interpret the headline as satire speaks to the depth of the disconnect between the climate religionists of the Biden administration and flyover America.

TRUCKERS

*The state and federal regulators collaborating on
this unrealistic patchwork of regulations have
no grasp on the real costs of designing, building,
manufacturing, and operating the trucks that
deliver their groceries, clothes, and goods.*

—Chris Spear, President and CEO, American
Trucking Associations, March 31, 2023

Truckers move America. They are essential actors in our economic ecosystem. Without them your grocery shelves are empty. Everyone with a blade of common sense understands these basic facts of life.

Nevertheless, in March 2023, the Biden EPA approved waivers under the Clean Air Act that gave states such as California the authority to implement heavy-duty vehicle and engine emission standards, i.e., an electric truck mandate (by 2035), thereby setting the stage for an economic showdown against the very people who bring food to our dinner tables.

Truckers are notoriously independent. They chafe at government regulation. They are entrepreneurial. And they especially hate high energy prices that accompany inflation. This latter point bears repeating. Higher fixed costs mean less take-home money for the same work.

More important—truckers understand electric trucks will not be viable alternatives to diesel in the near future. The technology simply does not exist. They further realize the prohibitive cost of "going electric" will drive some of them out of business. It's an economic reality of no special interest to the regulators in Sacramento and Washington, D.C.

THE BOTTOM LINE: Those who toy with the economic lifeblood of an economy will pay a high price in the end.

LAND GRAB

The 30 x 30 initiative is an extension of the top-down, central planning vision Washington bureaucrats hiding in federal agencies possess. D.C. bureaucrats believe they know what is best for rural America, all while they live in a concrete swamp completely detached from the producers who feed, fuel, and clothe our nation and the world.

—U.S. Sen. Kevin Cramer
(R-ND) April 22, 2022

The phrase "land grab" can be a pejorative depending on who's grabbing who's land. Still, it applies where the usual suspects set about to close off vast amounts of land in the interest of "climate change" (what else?).

The context here are two executive orders issued in the very early stages of the Biden administration. The first established a goal of "conserv[ing] at least 30 percent of our lands and waters by 2030" (the so-called "30 by 30" executive order). The order ran to fifty-seven pages.

The second (issued two weeks later) rescinded an earlier Department of Interior "secretarial order" that required prior approval by states and local subdivisions for federal land purchases. Here, local governments had the standing to contest controversial federal takings—as did the miners, farmers, and ranchers who rely on the land for their livelihoods.

Of course, there is a remarkable lack of scientific data to back up the anti-growth advocates' claim that such preservation efforts are required to mitigate climate change or protect certain species from extinction. That the case for the foregoing is usually accompanied by the typical emotional warnings of impending doom coming our way is the least shocking aspect of this initiative.

THE BOTTOM LINE: Beware preservationists bearing new executive orders.

BRIGHT LIGHTS

*The Department of Energy should be
focused on American energy independence,
not on what light bulbs you can or can't
purchase for your home or business.*

—U.S. Rep. Andy Barr (R-KY), August 1, 2023

*Let there be light! [just not as
bright as it used to be]*

—God

We now have a new Prince of Darkness—Joe Biden. His Department of Energy wants a nationwide ban on incandescent and similar-style halogen bulbs, which have dominated the lightbulb market for decades.

A similar proposal was under review in the Trump administration in 2019 before the president pulled the plug (so to speak). Mr. Trump concluded the juice (energy savings) was not worth the squeeze (increased cost). To boot, Fox News (not DJT's favorite cable outlet) reported that Mr. Trump thought the LED replacement bulbs too expensive—and that they gave him that orange tint so many lefty comedians find impossible to ignore.

Critics—including Republican members of Congress—criticized the move as yet another in a laundry list of progressive-inspired policies that will make life more expensive for the working class while resulting in minimal savings. Alas, the increasingly dire economic station of the deplorables is not a priority for the bi-coastal green crowd.

THE BOTTOM LINE: I never thought I'd see a black market in light bulbs—until the Biden administration came along.

BORDER LIVING

Unless you have been here and have lived here, you really have no idea how bad it is.... When you're on your own property and don't feel safe, it's really unnerving. It really is. But that's what we're dealing with down here. It's like nothing we have ever seen before. I really hope something can be done.

—Stephanie Crisp Canales, Texas rancher, on Biden-era instability at the southern border, June 23, 2021

Not enough has been written about the farmers and ranchers who live on the southern border. Their way of life has been demonstrably degraded by drug cartels allowed to conduct their dirty business on private property.

Testimonies too numerous to count speak to how the cartels' malign presence cuts into the rancher's/farmer's usable land—including the extraordinary expenses associated with damage to structures, pipelines, fences, and livestock.

But this is quantifiable damage. What is unquantifiable is the knowledge that the entirety of one's own land is not available because the U.S. government has decided it no longer cares to enforce its own border—that the diminution in value suffered by local landowners is a small price to pay for the promise of an open border.

The victims are typically fiercely independent ranchers/farmers/outdoorsmen with few woke sympathies and decidedly conservative values. They are accordingly of no value to progressive narrative makers. And so nobody cares to ask where this group goes to secure *their* social justice.

THE BOTTOM LINE: Loss of enjoyment of one's own land, and a concomitant loss of income, is just one more negative consequence of open borders.

WILDFIRES

I don't think anybody can deny the
impact of the climate crisis anymore.…
We've never seen this much fire.

—Biden presser on Hawaii wildfires and other
significant weather events, August 30, 2023

Americans are acclimated to climate religionists (especially politicians) linking every hurricane that rumbles up the East Coast in late summer to apocalyptic climate change. This despite numerous well-respected climate scientists opining that the frequency and intensity of the big storms have not changed a great deal over time. Indeed, the federal government's own data reflects no evidence to support an uptick in hurricane strength or intensity over the past 170 years.

Still, the terrible wildfires that devasted parts of Maui in early August 2023 provided yet another opportunity to connect climate to a natural catastrophe on U.S. soil.

But the nexus at the core of the green lobby's argument here is even more tenuous. Even legacy media reported expert opinion to the effect that wildfires are almost always human-caused events. The narrative was further diluted when reports surfaced of a wild grass species that authorities knew could act as an accelerant in a wildfire scenario and (of course) that local utility oversight may have valued "energy transition" over safety and mitigation efforts.

**THE BOTTOM LINE: Valuing energy transition
over public safety reflects the existential threat
that is present-day climate religion.**

MOOD SWINGS

*Some of the changes proposed by the
White House Office of Management
and Budget appeared to embed political
objectives in the analysis. That isn't*

*what benefit-cost analysis—required by
presidents for more than forty years and
increasingly by courts—is supposed to do.*

—Susan Dudley and W. Kip Viscusi, *Wall
Street Journal* op-ed, August 28, 2023

Of all the entrees contained herein, this one might be the most difficult to describe because…nobody truly knows what it means.

I refer to the proposed regulatory guidance issued by the White House in August 2023—an initiative purportedly intended to standardize the way in which federal agencies are to quantify cost-benefit analysis when drafting new regulations.

The new language requires regulators to measure potential impact (cost-benefit) on "ecosystem services," to ensure such impacts receive equal weight as compared to other, more traditional cost-benefit measurements. In this newly derived measurement space, the guidance requires quantification of "nonmaterial impacts" on human spirituality, cultural practices, or mental health. For example, federal transportation officials would be required to quantify the impact of a proposed new roads project…on a driver's *mental health* or, presumably, one's mood. It is accordingly easy to foresee a spiking demand for additional psychologist-regulators in the coming years.

Of course, there is no end to such a subjective process. But I guess that is the very point of the exercise.

THE BOTTOM LINE: Those who have never been employed in the private sector simply do not (and usually cannot) appreciate the heavy burden overregulation places on job creators.

FREEZIN' UP

*'A bunch of dead robots': How
freezing temps turned Tesla charging
stations into EV graveyards.*

—KTVZ News Channel 21
Chicago, February 12, 2024

While still a popular Christmas season classic, "Baby It's Cold Outside" is also a fitting moniker for Joe Biden's ill-fated foray into pretend environmental science circa 2024.

Well-chronicled problems associated with electric vehicle stations freezing up in cold weather were only part of the story. The more immediate issue started with the bosses at America's automobile unions who had become none too pleased with job cutbacks as a result of dwindling consumer demand for electric vehicles. This of course caught the attention of candidate Biden in the winter of 2024.

The result was a directive to the Environmental Protection Agency ordering a rollback of clean air regulations that had mandated two-thirds of all automobiles sold by 2032 be EVs. Screams of bloody murder by the environmental lobby were duly noted by a Biden campaign running neck and neck with Donald Trump in the critical, automobile-industry-dependent state of Michigan.

**THE BOTTOM LINE: For lefty politicians facing
difficult election seasons, problematic polls can
result in delayed virtue signaling. Jus' sayin'.**

THE SAGA OF LNG

*This moratorium on new permits is
expected to last after the 2024 elections
and therefore is easily characterized as
purely for domestic political aims.*

—Katie Klaber, *Pittsburgh Business
Times*, February 2024

The not-so-secret driver of America's emergence as an energy independent nation during the Trump era was the fracking/natural gas revolution. Talk about good things coming together at once: the arrival of new horizontal drilling technologies, a much cleaner-burning fossil fuel, a high-demand product in Europe and Africa, and a political leader willing to exploit America's natural resource advantage to the benefit of the American consumer—and, not incidentally, American labor.

One additional advantage was much discussed: no longer would American foreign policy decisions be based (or appear to be based) on the need to placate otherwise unfriendly, sometimes hostile regimes in order to keep Americans warm in winter and cool in summer.

And then the Biden administration paused pending LNG export permits, allegedly to "update the underlying analysis for authorizations on exports of LNG to non-free-trade-agreement countries"—an act widely interpreted as a sop to an environmental lobby anxious about Mr. Biden's lack of progress on green energy initiatives. A loss on July 1, 2024, a federal judge blocked the permitting suspension as violative of the Natural Gas Act and Administrative Procedure Act.

THE BOTTOM LINE: The Biden administration's attempts to placate the green energy lobby through administrative holdups, while ensuring grid reliability is mutually exclusive—a point not lost on America's voters.

NEXT UP: WASHERS AND DRYERS

*Another day, another regulation from the
Biden administration, to remove products
from the shelves and limit what people can
buy in the name of their ideological goals.
At this point, consumers have gotten the
message: If it moves or has a motor and
it is in your house, Biden would like it to
cost more and probably be less effective.*

—O.H. Skinner, Executive Director,
Alliance for Consumers

The more paranoid (and cynical) among us suspected Joe Biden's regulatory assault on the family household would not stop at gas stoves.

The cynics were proven correct when the Biden administration issued final regulations for "energy efficient" washers and dryers in March 2024. Indeed, it was open season on any and all household items that require electricity in order to work and, as always, the usual rationale was offered: reduction of carbon emissions and savings on water bills.

Yet, in a separate matter just a month earlier, the Fifth Circuit Court of Appeals noted that some "energy efficient" appliances pushed by the Biden administration require more energy and water than traditional appliances, a result seemingly antithetical to what the green appliances are supposed to deliver. But virtue signaling often beats hard science in the world of green advocacy.

THE BOTTOM LINE: Understand that the modern regulatory state never rests; it survives and multiplies.

ALASKA DREAMIN'

[The Biden administration] has imposed more sanctions on Alaska than [it] has on Iran.

—Senator Dan Sullivan (R-AL)

The environmental lobby's relentless campaign against American energy independence continued to take center stage during the 2024 campaign as the Biden administration further restricted fossil fuel development projects in Alaska's National Petroleum Reserve—land that had been set aside for oil and gas drilling by Congress a century ago. Nevertheless, the announcement included typical green virtue signaling: in this case, resisting resource development to honor the "culture, history, and enduring wisdom of Alaska natives." Alas, what went unacknowledged in the president's announcement were the local tribal leaders who stood in support of the local drilling.

Many on the right interpreted the move as more inconsistency from an administration at war with itself—one that is all about placating anti-development, anti-mining green interest groups while proclaiming the need to secure critical minerals required for use in EVs and computer chip production.

THE BOTTOM LINE: Four years later, Mr. Biden's hodgepodge of environmental programs proposes green-friendly goals that often stand in conflict with (free) market and (real) science realities both on the ground and *in* the ground.

DIRE PREDICTIONS

We don't have much more than ten years.

—President Joe Biden on the unfolding
global climate crisis, September 14, 2021

Guy walks into his doctor's office.
Doctor says you have six months to live.
Guy says he can't pay his bill.
Doctor gives him another six months.

—Comedian Henny Youngman

This oldie but goodie from Mr. Youngman highlights the easy negligence so often seen and heard from the climate warriors of the Biden administration. Easy because doomsday predictions regarding fossil fuels come so effortlessly for them. Negligent because they know support for huge data centers, advanced manufacturing facilities, and AI requires load growth far beyond present capacity—a void that alternatives are unable to fill given present technology. Add the significant environmental damage inflicted by alternatives and the massive taxpayer subsidies they require, and the whole house of cards comes to light.

Still, the need to virtue signal (often performed by liberal arts majors with little idea of what they are talking about) remains strong. So politicians continue to ignore market realities and hard science. Because they can….

THE BOTTOM LINE: A zealot-like belief in climate alarmism encourages the notion that alternatives are plentiful, reliable, and cheap—none of which is true in the real world at this time.

TAXPAYER ABUSE

*I find it rather startling…that the EPA
and the administration are not doing
any better research as to where our
American taxpayer dollars are going.*

—Senator Shelley Moore Capito (R-WV),
May 21, 2024

Kudos to Senator Shelley Moore Capito (R-WV) and the *Wall Street Journal* (May 23, 2024) for exposing one of the more ridiculous consequences from the terribly mislabeled and fraudulently marketed Inflation Reduction Act (IRA).

Indeed, the IRA was a classic DC swamp creature wherein the Biden administration threw in excess of $1 trillion at green subsidies (and green advocates) and labeled it an attempt to control Mr. Biden's self-created inflationary spiral. And so, $40 billion of taxpayer largesse was delivered to the Environmental Protection Agency (EPA), including $600 million for a grant program devoted to—you guessed it—"environmental justice."

One such grant recipient was the Climate Justice Alliance, an umbrella group of ninety progressive organizations allegedly all-in on the business of "environmental health and justice challenges."

THE BOTTOM LINE: No reader will be surprised to learn that the Climate Justice Alliance represents the front-line troops employed to fight on behalf of left-wing causes, including such climate-related issues as "Free Palestine" and the abolishment of U.S. Immigration and Customs Enforcement (ICE).

CHAPTER 6

FOREIGN POLICY

AFGHANISTAN I (WITHDRAWAL)

[The draw-down of U.S. forces will be] secure and orderly.... The likelihood there's going to be the Taliban overrunning everything and owning the whole country is highly unlikely.

—President Joe Biden, July 8, 2021

Truth be told, no U.S. administration has clean hands when it comes to this godforsaken country. Suffice to say more than a few occupying empires have had a terrible reckoning in what remains a generally ungovernable, tribal part of the world.

Still, the president's overnight decision to pull the plug on American military involvement will go down as one of his most infamous policy miscalculations. To wit: the decision contravened advice from his Commander of U.S. Forces–Afghanistan, the secretary of defense, and the chairman of the Joint Chiefs of Staff. Moreover, troop caps imposed by Biden necessitated the disastrous overnight withdrawal from Bagram

Air Force Base, resulting in the abandonment of billions of dollars of military hardware (airplanes, tanks, grenade launchers, mortars, Humvees, small arms, and millions of rounds of ammunition) as well as the abandonment of thousands of Afghan collaborators who would become immediate targets of the Taliban. And then there was the deadly attack at the Kabul Airport wherein thirteen U.S. service members and a hundred Afghans died amid a chaotic evacuation that conjured up terrible memories of the rooftop helicopter evacuation from the U.S. embassy in Saigon in 1975.

The U.S. spent more than $2 trillion in a failed twenty-year nation-building experiment in Afghanistan. There was precious little taxpayer accountability over that term. But the maintenance of 2,500 to 3,000 (in country) troops had long provided a foundation for a tenuous status quo that at least kept the Taliban at bay and Afghan girls in school. That is, until a new president decided to up and simply "turn the page." The historic disaster that followed will long be remembered by a country conflicted by prolonged military engagements in faraway hostile venues.

THE BOTTOM LINE: President Biden ignored the advice of his top generals in ordering the immediate overnight abandonment of Afghanistan.

AFGHANISTAN II (TAXPAYER MONEY)

*[It is] no longer a question of whether the
Taliban are diverting assistance from our*

*programs to help the Afghan people, but
rather how much they are diverting.*

—John Sopko, Special Inspector General
for Afghanistan Reconstruction,
report dated July 30, 2023

During the same week of August 2023 wherein families of the thirteen U.S. soldiers murdered in the chaotic withdrawal from Afghanistan marked the two-year anniversary of that fiasco, the Special Inspector General for Afghanistan Reconstruction reported that $2.35 billion of U.S. aid had flowed into the country since America's abrupt departure. The report further noted that another $1.70 billion remained in the pipeline for possible future disbursement.

The IG—who had previously made public his concerns about the ultimate diversion of U.S. aid—once again focused on the diversion of funds meant for relief and reconstruction efforts at a time when the Taliban was back to its old familiar tricks, including "extrajudicial killings," "crimes against humanity," and renewed efforts at "gender apartheid."

Here, history had yet again repeated itself: more waste of taxpayer money and the regression of the Taliban to seventh-century moral codes. Yet another foreign policy "success" in the eyes of Joe Biden.

THE BOTTOM LINE: At the very least, U.S. taxpayers deserve a thorough accounting of every red cent spent (including the cost of equipment left behind) as a result of our twenty-year military intervention in Afghanistan. But don't hold your breath.

AFGHANISTAN III (BETRAYAL)

*[Working with American and British troops
was the] biggest mistake of my life.*

—"Steve-O," code name of Afghan
interpreter left behind at Hamid Karzai
International Airport, August 2021

Numerous conservative media outlets reported on the thousands of Afghan allies (and a still unknown number of Americans) left behind to fend for themselves in the aftermath of America's sudden withdrawal from Afghanistan. These reports included efforts of former high-ranking American officers organizing rescue campaigns to save Afghan collaborators who had remained loyal to American civil authorities and the U.S. military.

And then an August 2023 United Nations report on the fate of our Afghan partners confirmed America's worst fears: a minimum of eight hundred known human rights "violations" (beatings, arbitrary arrests, torture, murders) committed by Taliban enforcers.

As the manhunts continue, the Taliban government's now two-year-old assurances to Mr. Biden regarding safe passage for Afghan collaborators rings more hollow than ever.

**THE BOTTOM LINE: No wonder the Biden administration
does everything in its power to suppress coverage
of this (continuing) foreign policy disaster.**

AFGHANISTAN IV (TERRORISTS)

As of February 2022, the National Ground Intelligence Center (NGIC) had identified at least fifty Afghan military-age male evacuees— none of whom was [a special immigrant visa] applicant—who had been flagged as significant security risks by the Defense Department. By August 2022, that number had risen to sixty-five.

—Jerry Dunleavy and James Hasson in *Kabul: The Untold Story of Biden's Fiasco and the American Warriors Who Fought to the End*

In August of 2023, the above-cited book was released. Contained therein was another bombshell pertaining to our disastrous withdrawal from Afghanistan and our notoriously porous southern border: An undetermined number of terrorists who had left fingerprints on IEDs (improvised explosive devices) targeted to kill American soldiers were among the thousands of Afghan refugees the Biden administration allowed into the U.S. after the evacuation of Kabul. Recall these were the same flights that left behind American citizens and Afghans who had cooperated with us. Media reports alleged the men had disappeared into the interior of the U.S. and would prove quite difficult to track down.

THE BOTTOM LINE: Rarely do two major policy catastrophes come together in such a dangerous way, but the Biden administration is capable of spectacular failure. And here we are.

CHINA I

*China is going to eat our lunch? Come on,
man.... They're not competition for us.*

—Candidate Joe Biden, May 2, 2019

*I don't want to contain China.... I just want
to make sure that we have a relationship
with China that is on the up-and-up, squared
away. Everybody knows what it's all about.*

—President Joe Biden, September 10, 2023

Engagement and indulgence toward Xi Jinping and the CCP have characterized Washington's uni-party approach to China for the last thirty-five years. This bipartisan strategy was all about opening American business opportunities to one and a half billion new potential customers, and don't worry so much about the Tiananmen Square massacre and Uyghur concentration camps and South China Sea artificial island building and Confucius spy operations on American campuses and relentless theft of our intellectual property and Hong Kong's suppression of human rights and the true origins of Covid-19 and that "silly balloon" that traversed the U.S. and Beijing's relentless saber-rattling over the Republic of China, Taiwan. That bipartisan but now discredited party line—that the communist Chinese would inevitably adopt capitalism and democratize—had been Joe Biden's refrain for over four decades. His ascendancy to the presidency would mark more of the same.

This much was crystal clear after an embarrassing initial meeting in Alaska between Secretary of State Tony Blinken and China's top diplomat Yang Jiechi. In that encounter Mr. Yang at various times cited the uncertainty surrounding the U.S. presidential election results of 2020, the repeated failure of neocon-inspired military misadventures around the world, and how "Black Lives Matter" merely represents the latest chapter of race discrimination in the good ol' U.S. of A. Here, woke was thrown right back in the face of the Biden administration *by the Chinese communists.* In other words, a brutal totalitarian regime utilized the organs and language of progressivism as a sledgehammer against a feckless Biden State Department. Score another loss for Foggy Bottom's weak and woke program of appeasement.

THE BOTTOM LINE: The Chinese feared the "cowboy" Ronald Reagan. Likewise the unpredictable disrupter from Queens. Any bet as to where they fall on Tony Blinken and Joe Biden?

CHINA II (FILL'ER UP)

China is the primary customer of Iranian oil
and purchases other sanctioned goods from
Iran, such as petrochemicals and metals.

—Saaed Ghasseminejad, Defense of
Democracies Policy Brief, May 6, 2024

Not so long ago, the Obama administration—desperate for a legacy peace deal—sent the Iranians planes full of cash in order to buy time on the mullah's nuclear development program. All the while, Mr. Obama looked the other way while Iran funneled the money into developing its ballistic missile program and its terror network proxies. (Note that Hezbollah alone has fired thousands of missiles into northern Israel since Obama left office.)

Now fast forward to the Biden administration's propensity to cite "tough" sanctions against Iran while simultaneously looking the other way as Beijing became a major purchaser of Iranian oil—and funder of its military machine.

Here then was a perfect resolution for the wobbly Mr. Biden and two of the world's most notorious regimes. Biden (and Tony Blinken) get to talk tough about his sanctions regime while ignoring oil-dependent China's move to fill the mullah's pockets—a risk-free gambit by Xi Jinping in light of Biden's persistent desire to lower the temperature with Beijing.

THE BOTTOM LINE: There is nothing the Biden administration can point to that has made the Middle East a safer or more secure place. Indeed, two of the world's most dangerous regimes have only been strengthened by America's weakness on the world stage.

ISRAEL I (ANTAGONIST)

This is one of the most extreme Cabinets I've seen, and I go back to Golda Meier.

—President Joe Biden on the makeup of Prime Minister Benjamin Netanyahu's government, July 9, 2023

A relatively new but now firmly established plank of the progressive agenda seeks to challenge right-wing Israeli governments—especially when led by Bibi Netanyahu. Whether the issue was judicial reform or West Bank autonomy or security operations in Gaza (prior to the Hamas-led terrorist invasion from Gaza in October 2023), the Biden administration happily and gratuitously took shots at Netanyahu's most recent administration.

The strategy entails few political risks. Democrats continue to count on two-thirds of the Jewish vote come election day, despite progressive antipathy toward Israeli security concerns (and Israel generally). As some left-leaning Jewish Democrats move toward less engagement with Israel, ascendant progressives (some with pro-Palestinian views, as was observed in the aftermath of Hamas's October 7, 2023, invasion of southern Israel) continue to take full advantage.

Biden administration policy regarding the entire Middle East is similarly misguided. The president's antagonism toward Saudi Arabia and wistful desire to revive the terribly flawed nuclear deal with the mullahs in Tehran damaged our relationships with the same Sunni allies that President Trump had successfully cajoled into quiet cooperation with Israel.

Israel is of course nervous that its mortal enemy Iran (friend and funder of Hamas, Hezbollah, and the Yemenite Houthis) will soon join the nuclear club. There could be few more destabilizing events in the always dangerous melting pot that is the Middle East.

THE BOTTOM LINE: One of the Biden administration's first acts was to remove the Houthis from the Foreign Terrorist Organization (FTO) and Specially Designated Global Terrorist (SDGT) lists. Here, another example of Biden-era appeasement toward the mullahs in Tehran that has empowered

terror-friendly Iran at the expense of our ally Israel. Chalk up two more Biden administration foreign policy failures.

ISRAEL II (INVASION)

Biden in Rehoboth Beach this weekend after high-stakes week responding to Israel crisis

—*Delaware News Journal*
headline, October 20, 2023

Twelve days after the murderous Hamas-sponsored invasion of Israel on October 7, 2023, Joe Biden gave only his second prime-time national address from the Oval Office. But there was one problem: the fifteen-minute talk was more about the need to rearm Ukraine than the savage terror attacks that brought an already destabilized Israel-Palestinian relationship to the brink of yet another Middle East war.

The speech ignored Iran's sponsorship of Hamas in Gaza and Hezbollah in Lebanon and the Houthis in Yemen. It instead amounted to an omnibus funding request for yet another $60 billion for Ukraine, $14 billion for Israel, $14 billion to process migrants showing up at our southern border, $10 billion for general humanitarian aid, and $100 million in humanitarian assistance for Gaza—money that would be handed over regardless of American hostages held by Hamas. Hamas in turn promised the White House that the aid money would not be stolen…like it usually is. And the White House and the State Department believed them…as they usually do.

Okay, you say, it's just the expected negligence and naivete of the Biden White House. But the prior day had witnessed the accidental doxing of U.S. Special Forces personnel when that same White House posted uncensored photos of Mr. Biden with our most elite soldiers in Israel.

THE BOTTOM LINE: Iran's foreign currency reserves have increased from $6 billion to $60 billion during the Biden years. American indifference to our own sanctions on Iranian oil sales is the primary reason for all that additional currency that helps fund Iranian terror campaigns around the world— especially Hamas's and Hezbollah's terror wars against Israel.

ISRAEL III (GAZA...AND MICHIGAN)

The State of Israel will not cease fire. We will destroy Hamas and continue to fight until the last of the hostages is returned home.

—Israel Katz, Israeli Foreign Minister

Joe Biden, the reliably liberal, reliably pro-Israel senator from Delaware, represented the mainstream of what was then a liberal labor political party for forty years. Then a hyper-progressive, not-so-pro-Zionist movement took control of his party. America's relationship with Tel Aviv has not been the same since.

The foregoing came full circle as concurrent events battered Biden's reelection campaign—the political desire to placate pro-Palestinian Muslim Democrats in the must-win swing state of Michigan and the equally sudden unease Jewish Democrats felt in the aftermath of America's abstention on a UN Security Council resolution. Said resolution called for the immediate cessation of fighting during the Muslim holy month of Ramadan, an immediate and unconditional release of all hostages, and the lifting of all barriers regarding the importation of humanitarian assistance.

Mr. Biden's Security Council gambit signaled a significant policy departure from the previous Biden position, one that had included three consecutive vetoes of Security Council resolutions calling for an immediate cease fire. In the immediate aftermath of the resolution's passage, Prime Minister Netanyahu canceled a high-level Israeli delegation that was scheduled to fly to Washington for talks.

THE BOTTOM LINE: The Biden administration's initial high-profile pivot away from Israel only created more uncertainty as to America's reliability in the perpetually unstable cauldron that is the Middle East.

ISRAEL IV (BETRAYAL)

Biden vows to cut off weapons if
Israel tries to finish off Hamas.

—*New York Post*, May 9, 2024

As domestic protests against Israel's military operations in Gaza grew into 1960s-esque campus riots/encampments and American Muslims continued to assert their political leverage against the Biden administration, the president began to withhold weapons and ordinance deliveries to an Israeli Defense Forces (IDF) that had begun a final push into Rafah, the last Hamas stronghold in Gaza. The stunning move appeared to catch Mr. Netanyahu's government off guard despite repeated warnings from Biden administration officials (and Biden himself) to delay the Rafah campaign.

Here then was a classic "caught between a rock and a hard place" scenario for a stumbling Biden candidacy: continue to bleed Muslim support by giving Israel what it needed to complete the job in Gaza, or withhold congressionally approved weapons deliveries that could endanger the mission and raise the ire of Jewish Democrats.

Mr. Biden, battered and trailing in the polls, sought a middle path in an unsurprising move to those who had been paying attention. A reliably consistent, supportive approach to Bibi Netanyahu's government has never been a Biden strong suit.

In typical fashion, Mr. Netanyahu assured his country that the IDF would carry out the Rafah initiative to its conclusion, with or without U.S. munitions.

THE BOTTOM LINE: Your mom always said that trying to have it both ways never works. Your mom was right....

IRAN I

There is no such thing as a gentleman's agreement with the Islamic Republic.

—Behnam Ben Taleblu, Senior
Fellow, Foundation for Defense of
Democracies, June 30, 2023

A quiet policy success of the Trump administration was the "maximum pressure" policy instituted against the world's most notorious sponsor of terror. The campaign of crippling sanctions against oil sales and aggressive isolation proved disruptive to the Iranian economy—and raised the temperature on the Iranian street. It also helped sustain a disruptive social environment that had the mullahs more preoccupied with their restive population than engaged in undermining their archenemy, Israel.

And then the fledgling Biden administration jettisoned what was working in favor of Obama-era diplomatic reengagement, including a backdoor restart to negotiations over the flawed 2015 nuclear accord between Iran and the West and the loosening of sanctions targeting illegal oil exports (which hit a five-year high under the Biden administration).

On September 11, 2023 (of all days), Biden announced a deal wherein America would unfreeze $6 billion of Iranian oil money held in a South Korean bank and release five Iranian prisoners in exchange for five American hostages. Iran took maximum advantage of its unexpected new leverage—including accelerating its nuclear program and doubling down on its status as a regional obstacle to peace in the Middle East. (To wit: Iranian backing of the bloody Hamas-led invasion from the Gaza Strip in October 2023.) One can only imagine the longer-term takeaway the world's most notorious sponsor of terrorism derives from highly lucrative kidnappings that garner billions for the regime from an always indulgent Biden administration.

THE BOTTOM LINE: Obama/Kerry/Biden foreign policy misadventures in the Middle East continue to pay dividends for the despotic autocrats in Tehran.

IRAN II (THE HOUTHIS)

*The Sa'id al-Jamal network relies on a web of
exchange houses based throughout the Middle
East to facilitate the movement of Iranian funds
to Houthis-aligned financial firms in Yemen.*

—U.S. Department of the Treasury
Press Release, December 28, 2023

Iran's malign presence in the Middle East is an unfortunate fact of life. But the miscreant regime's nefarious actions grew evermore dangerous after the latest Hamas-Israel war began on October 7, 2023.

To wit, Iran's funding and support for localized terror groups took on a more formalized role when Islamic Revolutionary Guard Corps operatives began to transfer more intelligence and reconnaissance to Houthi rebel forces attempting to disrupt international trade on the Red Sea.

Per the usual Biden modus operandi, U.S. and allied forces conducted sporadic military and cyber attack operations in response. Republicans and military analysts from the Hudson Institute and other right-leaning think tanks bemoaned the limited nature of the responses that had little, if any, deterrent impact. Indeed, Houthi leadership kept directing drone and missile attacks against commercial shipping, which required shipping companies to redirect their routes around the threat.

THE BOTTOM LINE: Funny how basic economics so often comes into play when dissecting Biden foreign policy. In this instance, an unwillingness to confront the root cause of Middle East instability led to extended travel times for commercial

shippers, which in turn led to higher transportation costs, which in turn contributed to persistent inflation and higher prices at the grocery store for American consumers.

IRAN III (PINPRICKS AND POLITICS)

Peace is not the absence of war....

—Baruch Spinoza, *Theologico-Political Treatise*, 1670

The West has put up with Iranian saber-rattling and terror funding for decades. The former is by now familiar: death to the great Satan (America) and the junior Satan (Israel). The talk has been backed up by money and intelligence sharing with its proxy armies, including Hamas, Hezbollah, and Islamic jihad. Their willingness to wreak havoc in Gaza, in northern Israel, and on the Red Sea has occasioned dozens of pinprick responses from the U.S. and its Sunni allies.

Many of these responses are not only limited by design but are signaled in advance to the opposition (such as the Iranian missile barrage aimed at Israel proper and the Israeli response aimed at Iran proper in April 2024) in order to avoid a wider conflict.

It is true that these self-limiting moves have prevented a wider Middle Eastern war in the short term. But it is equally true that each chapter of missile and drone tit for tat escalates the stakes—such as the above example wherein the attacks were lodged against the actual combatant nation states and not proxies.

This slow but steady proliferation exercise reflects the understandable fear of a major conflict but also reveals Biden-era weakness in dealing with the ever-dangerous provocations of the region's destabilizing actors.

THE BOTTOM LINE: The Biden decision to back off the Trump era's "maximum pressure" campaign has empowered the world's most notorious sponsor of terror to increase its disruptive campaigns throughout the Middle East. The mullahs of Tehran are surely thankful for the reprieve.

DIGITAL AMBASSADOR

*Navy leadership knew this was a ridiculous
and embarrassing stunt, and that is why they
initially denied involvement with the program.*

—U.S. Rep. Jim Banks (R-IN), May 9, 2023

One need not speculate as to how the Biden Pentagon's fixation on race, sex, and gender over mission have impacted military recruitment goals: Biden-era shortfalls say it all. Here, the promotion of a "non-binary" drag queen social media influencer/officer to be a "digital ambassador" (and the face of a recruitment drive) proved to be the latest chapter of woke-gone-wrong. My (First Marine Division Korea) dad could never have imagined such an unserious approach to our national security challenges.

The taxpayers can only hope this iteration of Pentagon marketing foolishness will be a one-and-done, never-to-be-revisited experiment. (The Navy says its digital ambassador program was a pilot that ended in March 2023.)

Those same taxpayers should expect a new GOP administration to identify the person/office who thought this type of messaging would be a tonic for what ails our military. Until then, we can only speculate on the glee emanating from our enemies around the world.

THE BOTTOM LINE: Military recruitment should be the last place on earth for woke advertising. Full Stop.

HUNTER

No one f…s with a Biden.

—President Joe Biden, hot-mic
comment caught during official visit
to Florida, October 5, 2022

*Democrats Say It'll Take A Lot More Than
Eyewitness Testimony, Bank Records, Audio,
Video, Complete Confessions For Them
To Believe Biden Did Anything Wrong.*

—Headline in *The Babylon
Bee*, August 10, 2023

Family members should typically be off-limits when discussing a national administration. But first son Hunter Biden is the exception when it comes to disreputable behavior conducted in close proximity to political power.

For present purposes, there is no reason to regurgitate the many questionable chapters of Hunter's business dealings with friendly and not-so-friendly foreign governments while his father held the two most powerful positions in the world. The whys and wherefores of that relationship are and will be the stuff of *New York Times* bestsellers (and Congressional oversight hearings) for many years to come.

What *is* most disquieting about the never-ending Hunter storylines is the whopper told by the president in that famous October 22, 2020, presidential debate wherein he categorically denied that Hunter had ever made any money from Chinese interests. We now know that once Hunter's sweetheart plea deal fell apart, he admitted that commencing in 2017 he was paid $664,000 from Hudson West, a company he established with a partner with links to the Chinese energy company CEFC and the Chinese Communist Party. We also know (thanks to GOP House investigators) that Hunter's Chinese business partners sent $250,000 to Joe Biden's Delaware address in 2019.

To boot: The *Washington Post, New York Post* and Politico reported that Hunter made millions from 2014 on, primarily from "Chinese or Ukrainian interests." That even the reliably left-wing *Post* would give Mr. Biden four Pinocchios for his debate statement (albeit three years later) is noteworthy.

Similarly disquieting is the nonchalant manner the president employs whenever yet another Hunter payday from a foreign government story pops up on the newswires. The president's blank stare, shallow smirk, and detached demeanor are by now familiar and disarmingly effective—especially in light of a spectacularly heretofore uncurious media. Hey, if it's working, why change it?

THE BOTTOM LINE: It makes no difference whether Vice President Biden knew or simply did not wish to know about Hunter's business model—either is clearly unacceptable.

UKRAINE I (A THREAT)

*I'm leaving in six hours. If the prosecutor
is not fired, you're not getting the money.
Well, son of a bitch, he got fired.*

—Vice President Joe Biden at the Council
on Foreign Relations, January 23, 2018

This one was out in the open from the jump. It was Mr. Biden himself who famously threatened the Ukrainian government that he would withhold American foreign aid—$1 billion in loan guarantees—if Prosecutor General Viktor Shokin was not fired and thereby stopped from investigating corruption within the natural gas company Burisma. The company had previously employed Hunter Biden to the tune of $83,000 a month despite his lack of expertise/experience in the energy field.

THE BOTTOM LINE: That Mr. Shokin was fired within ninety days of the vice president's threat is a matter of record—as is Mr. Biden's arrogant and often replayed recollection about the firing as related to the Council on Foreign Relations.

UKRAINE II (ACCOUNTABILITY)

As long as it takes.

—President Biden on America's commitment
to Ukraine in its war with Russia, June 8, 2023

The definition of "it" is all important here. Does "it" mean reclaiming all the territory lost in the latest Russian incursion?

Does "it" mean reclaiming all of the land (including Crimea) lost to Russia since 2008? Or does "it" mean using the war to achieve regime change in Russia? No one is quite sure of the answer. But if "strategic ambiguity" is the goal here…it seems to be working as the American people remain confused.

What is not working is transparency. America has contributed tens of billions of dollars to the Ukrainian war effort (generally supported by a majority of Democrats and Republicans) in what amounts to a blank check as the taxpaying public has never been shown the books. (Some congressional Republicans have complained, but to no avail.)

The logical takeaway is that the Biden Pentagon deems the public dissemination of Ukraine-related expenditures irrelevant. In other words, that communication with the American public is on a "need to know" basis when it comes to the details of taxpayer dollars going to a foreign government known for its history of corruption.

THE BOTTOM LINE: The Biden administration has placed American taxpayers on the hook for the never-ending Ukraine-Russia War freight, and transparency be damned. Just one more reason flyover types are so cynical about this particular foreign engagement.

POWER VACUUMS

Whenever evil wins, it is only by default, by the moral failure of those who evade the fact that there can be no compromise on basic principles.

—Ayn Rand in *Capitalism: The Unknown Ideal*

Here's the real problem: You've created a
power vacuum in the criminal universe.
And nature abhors a vacuum.

—George Stacey in *The Spectacular Spider-Man*

When America's foreign policy goes wobbly…power vacuums occur. These black holes in turn invite the world's miscreants to do miscreant things.

Alas, there is no better practitioner of wobbly than Joe Biden. Indeed, the former senator and vice president may have been wrong on just about every major foreign policy call over the past forty years (per former Obama Defense Secretary Robert Gates), but he's outdone himself as America's forty-sixth president.

Here, Biden's lack of clarity regarding NATO's likely response should Vladimir Putin limit his latest Ukrainian invasion to a "minor incursion" helped spark a major European war with no end in sight. Here, Mr. Biden added to the Obama–Biden-era gift of airplanes full of cash delivered to the Iranian mullahs with the repeal of "maximum pressure" *and* the unfreezing of $6 billion of oil money as part of a hostage (shakedown) negotiation. Here, a new Biden administration renewed a yearly aid package to the Palestinian Liberation Organization (through the United Nations)—a handout that Mr. Trump had stopped in 2018. Here, a weak, woke, and indulgent Biden-Blinken foreign policy team was regularly mocked by the murderous dictator Xi Jinping as he amped up an increasingly aggressive saber-rattling campaign against Taiwan.

THE BOTTOM LINE: It takes a long time to crawl out of a power vacuum. Such will be the primary foreign policy legacy of Joe Biden.

UNESCO

[Withdrawal from UNESCO] reflects U.S. concerns with mounting arrears…the need for fundamental reform in the organization, and continuing anti-Israel bias…

—Heather Nauert, State Department spokeswoman, October 12, 2017

In December of 2023, only two months removed from the Hamas-sponsored terror attacks on October 7, 2023, the Biden administration marked (celebrated) America's return to membership in the United Nations Educational, Scientific and Cultural Organization (UNESCO).

The move was yet another repudiation of Trump-era policy. In 2018, Trump had withdrawn American membership—as Ronald Reagan did in 1984—due to the organization's well-established antipathy toward Israel and the fact that U.S. law prohibits taxpayer dollars from funding any U.N.-affiliated entity that admits the Palestinian Authority as a full member. Per published reports, a temporary waiver included in an omnibus bill enabled the president to bypass the prohibition.

Observers noted a number of rationales for the move, including a desire to counter China's growing influence within the organization. But conservatives pointed to UNESCO's recent focus on a misinformation/disinformation/hate-speech/

conspiracy-theory initiative as an especially attractive reason for the reunion. In this respect, the Biden administration had found yet another partner in its never-ending quest to corral speech that contravenes the administration's narratives:

THE BOTTOM LINE: A total of $619 million in taxpayer dollars (representing previously unpaid dues) will fund an organization that does nothing to further American interests around the world. And the beat goes on…

ISRAEL-MORAL EQUIVALENCE: UNFORESEEN CONSEQUENCES

Israel has done more to prevent civilian casualties in war than any military in history… setting a standard that will be both hard and potentially problematic to repeat.

—John Spencer, Chair of Urban
Warfare Studies, West Point

In January 2021, the incoming Biden administration rescinded Trump-era executive orders left and right because it could. Everything pertaining to the Trump administration *had* to be repealed.

One such rescission removed Trump's EO that called for sanctions against anyone participating in International Criminal Court (ICC) actions brought against citizens of a non-signatory nation (such as the U.S. and Israel). Note that Biden made the move against the backdrop of bipartisan congressional opposition to ICC prosecutions.

On May 21, 2024, ICC prosecutor Karim Khan made known his plan to seek arrest warrants against three of Hamas' leaders as well as Israeli Prime Minister Bibi Netanyahu and his Defense Minister Yoav Gallant for "war crimes" and "crimes against humanity." In other words, leaders of a notorious terror organization that raped, pillaged, and murdered innocent Israelis on October 7, 2023, were to be accorded the same treatment as the leaders of a western style democracy engaged in a brutal war to root out a terror army living on its border. Alas, the actions of a rigged, anti-Israel court were par for the course. Israelis have become accustomed to such treatment.

THE BOTTOM LINE: We have seen this depressing movie before: a knee-jerk move to reverse Trump-era policy backfires with negative consequences for American foreign policy.

CHAPTER 7

HEALTH AND HUNGER

FOOD STAMPS

Data show the Biden administration's overreach led to massive spikes in grocery prices. They're feeding inflation, not stopping hunger.

—Jonathan Ingram, Vice President of Policy and Research, Foundation for Government Accountability, statement to Fox News, August 24, 2023

The math is not difficult: a growing economy and low inflation mean fewer people in need of food stamps (aka the Supplemental Nutritional Assistance Program), while slower growth and spiking inflation mean more people on our welfare rolls.

The latter condition prevailed during the Biden era, and so the food stamp program expanded accordingly. In fact, per the Heritage Foundation, expansion of the program through new enrollees, increased benefits, and added administration costs doubled its total cost from $60 billion in 2019 under President Trump to $120 billion in FY 22 under President Biden.

That a major element in the rapidly increasing cost of the program was the Biden administration's 27 percent hike in benefits in 2021 is a matter of record—as is the end around executed by Mr. Biden in order to bypass congressional approval of the dramatic increase.

THE BOTTOM LINE: Biden economic policy was a three-part failure: 1. spiking inflation exposed consumers to dramatic increases in the cost of living; 2. relentless spending led to burgeoning annual budget increases; and 3. dramatic growth in the food stamp program made for yet further expansion of the modern welfare state.

OBAMACARE'S TARIFFS

Estimates from the Centers for Medicare & Medicaid Services, the nonpartisan Congressional Budget Office, and even the left-leaning Urban Institute have shown that the proliferation of STLDI plans leads to a net decline in the number of uninsured Americans.

—House Ways and Means Committee health blog, July 7, 2020

From the jump, Obamacare suffered from twin foundational challenges: its options were loaded down with expensive mandates ("essential benefits") that spiked premiums, and its (by design) inability to charge premiums as a function of age and medical condition.

One Trump-era fix was to encourage basic, no-frills Short-Term Limited-Duration Insurance (STLDI) plans that were inexpensive and thereby attractive to young, healthy consumers. But the removal of these low-cost members from the exchanges meant more red ink for Obamacare plans because of more expensive risk pools.

The Biden administration's response was par for the course: rulemaking that would serve to freeze the expansion of Trump's "skinny" benefit plans. Requiring young and healthy consumers to purchase benefits they do not need is classic Washington one-size-fits-all thinking, and yet another chapter in the never-ending campaign to prop up the hollowed Obamacare.

THE BOTTOM LINE: Yet another revealing but unsurprising example of what results when bureaucrats are empowered to limit consumer choice in the healthcare marketplace.

CHAPTER 8

HOUSING

MORTGAGE FEES

It's unprecedented. My email is full from mortgage companies and CEOs [telling] me how unbelievably shocked they are by this move.

—David Stevens, former CEO, Mortgage Bankers Association, April 16, 2023

The housing/mortgage crisis of 2008 resulted from a variety of causes, including Wall Street greed and political pressures brought to bear by left-leaning community activists against banks to underwrite so-called subprime loans. A common theme to emerge from that disaster: "Lesson learned…we will henceforth be careful about letting politics interfere with sound underwriting practices."

Alas, lessons allegedly learned are easily forgotten in the Biden era as the Federal Housing Administration (in the summer of 2023) floated a rule that sought to impose a fee on good-credit borrowers in order to subsidize poor-credit borrowers.

The proposed rationale: to provide "equitable and sustainable access to homeownership" per the FHA.

The Heritage Foundation estimated that borrowers with sound credit histories would pay an additional $15,000 during the life of a typical mortgage loan. If this initiative reminds you of the student loan forgiveness proposal, go to the head of the class.

THE BOTTOM LINE: Seems there is no end to the Biden administration's desire to make success more expensive, regardless of economic sector.

LOCAL ZONING

President Biden is calling on Congress to enact an innovative new competitive grant program that awards flexible and attractive funding to jurisdictions that take concrete steps to eliminate [exclusionary zoning].

—White House Fact Sheet accompanying $2.3 trillion infrastructure bill

Anti-growth advocates are lately all about federalizing local land use zoning. And they are not afraid to say it out loud. The stated goal of yet another front in the campaign to federalize everything is to outlaw "exclusionary zoning"—also known as single-family households—the very foundation of the housing market.

Progressives know this is not an easy sell. Local land use has always been the purview of local government—the better to hold local politicians accountable for local development. And then there's that old American dream of home ownership, still a go-to applause line between the coasts.

And so progressives do what they do well: weaponize speech. Here, roads and bridges become "racist," "suburban sprawl" becomes the mortal enemy, and "single-family housing" becomes the devil himself. Conversely, "affordable housing" is always laudable—$213 billion worth in Joe Biden's grandiose infrastructure bill.

THE BOTTOM LINE: That the loudest advocates of federal preemption rarely live in the most impacted communities is ironic and certainly inconvenient for the narrative. Gated communities are more their cup of tea. But no matter. Progressives know what is best for the common folk—just ask them.

MAUI

No comment.

—President Joe Biden at Rehoboth Beach,
Delaware, when questioned about the death
toll and unfolding federal response in the wake
of Maui's deadly wildfires, August 14, 2023

In this day and age, there *has* to be somebody in charge of optics in the Biden White House. But you wouldn't know it by the timing of the announcement of another $200 million of taxpayer money going to the war in Ukraine on the same day hundreds of suddenly homeless citizens of Maui were promised a one-time $700 payment in the immediate aftermath of wildfires that ravaged the beautiful island.

But there was more. The president would not disrupt his latest summer vacation. And so it took thirteen days before he could find the time to visit the devastation. Once there, he proceeded to insult the victims by comparing a small lightening-induced kitchen fire at his Washington, D.C., home years ago to the killer wildfires. This in addition to an attempted joke about how hot the ground was ("You guys catch the boots out here? That's a hot ground, man."). And then the mispronunciation of the names of multiple Hawaiian public officials during media availabilities. All in all, a public relations disaster on top of the horrific natural one.

THE BOTTOM LINE: How many unforced errors can one White House commit in the course of one catastrophe? Answer: More than you might imagine.

ONLY MIGRANTS NEED APPLY

I guess I should be flattered if people are coming because I'm the nice guy—that's the reason why it's happening—that I'm a decent man, or however it's phrased. That's why they are coming, because they know Biden's a good guy.

—President Joe Biden, March 25, 2021

A recurring theme of Biden administration policy is support for the millions of migrants who showed up at our southern border in response to the overturning of Trump-era policies such as "Stay in Mexico" and Title 42 Covid restrictions. Indeed, even the anguished cries of blue-city mayors suffering from an influx of unskilled migrants did little to quell Mr. Biden's preference for lax border policies.

Amid the chaos brought about by millions of uninvited new arrivals, one issue in particular garnered the administration's attention: migrant housing. And it was here that Biden policy was most active. To wit: a funding request to Congress (part of a larger, $40 billion funding request) that would provide temporary housing for migrants who had illegally crossed the border. The better to provide relief to local shelters stretched to the brim with the unending flow of migrants since January 2021.

That this initiative was brought forth during a time of historic homelessness suffered by record numbers of American citizens (especially veterans) was not lost on many observers left to wonder how government priorities could have become so misplaced in so brief a period of time.

THE BOTTOM LINE: A government that subsidizes housing for illegal migrants will produce more illegal migrants.

CHAPTER 9

IMMIGRATION

REMAIN IN MEXICO

> *The statistics show the exact opposite result that*
> *[DHS Secretary Alejandro Mayorkas] swore*
> *his policies were going to produce.… There are*
> *fewer arrests and fewer serious criminals being*
> *arrested.… If [Mayorkas] was really concerned*
> *about getting criminals off the street and out*
> *of the country, and he's seen two-plus years of*
> *the opposite result, wouldn't he change them?*
>
> —John Fabbricatore, former ICE
> Field Office Director, in testimony
> to Congress, July 13, 2023

Some on the right conveniently forget that the Trump administration had a less than successful start to southern border enforcement in 2017–2018. The situation on the ground only began to turn around in January 2019 with the adoption of a "Stay in Mexico" (migrant protection protocol) process wherein the Department of Homeland Security began requiring newly arriving migrants to remain in Mexico until their U.S. immigration court date.

The new status quo and generally quiet border remained until the Biden administration reversed the policy, in effect reinstituting a catch-and-release process whereby newly arriving migrants were released into the interior of the U.S. (while awaiting an immigration court hearing) if no other country accepted them for deportation.

As a direct result of this policy reversal, America has experienced a tidal wave of illegal immigration. U.S. Customs and Border Protection reported 1.95 million "enforcement actions" in fiscal 2021, another 2.76 million in fiscal 2022, and another 3.20 million by the end of fiscal 2023. As of January 1, 2024, total Biden-era migrant encounters exceeded 8 million, with 1.5 million (600,000 in fiscal 2023 alone) so-called "got-aways"—migrants that have crossed over the border without immigration officials knowing who they are or their reason for migrating here.

THE BOTTOM LINE: Immigration and Customs Enforcement (ICE) arrests of illegal migrants who have previous criminal records decreased 65 percent from 2018 to 2022. Per Mr. Fabbricatore's above-cited testimony, it appears mass immigration during the Biden years was indeed planned, with little regard to impacts on American towns, cities, and states.

TITLE 42

*What they did in December in anticipation
of the Title 42 ruling that never came
down was yet another act of enforcement*

*theater that jeopardizes public safety
and the integrity of our system.*

—R. J. Hauman, Government Relations,
Federation for American Immigration
Reform, January 25, 2023

On the heels of the scheduled lapse of Title 42 pandemic health restrictions, the Biden Department of Homeland Security released 515 migrants with criminal records and another 641 who were facing criminal charges from DHS facilities. Their release was made in order to secure additional detention space prior to the expected border surge. That the expected surge did not occur [the Supreme Court ordered that Title 42 be held in place while awaiting oral arguments on the constitutionality of the statute's restrictions] did not mitigate the damage. Per the *Washington Times*, besides the released convicts and those facing criminal charges, the Border Patrol had previously been instructed to refrain from making additional arrests.

We may never really know how many *new* criminal offenses (and of course new victims) have been generated by the newly emancipated offenders. But we *do* know that the general chaos at the border in combination with negligent planning around the termination of Title 42 made the country more unsafe. Note: Alleged Border Czar (and Vice President) Kamala Harris was nowhere to be seen as the foregoing events unfolded.

THE BOTTOM LINE: Enforcement theater has been the cornerstone of Biden immigration policy, the long-term consequences of which will be felt by American citizens/taxpayers for decades to come.

CHILDREN

*If nothing continues to be done, there
will be a catastrophic event.*

—Jallyn Sualog, former career Health and
Human Services staffer, in a 2021 email
on the Biden administration's failure to
protect unaccompanied migrant children
from trafficking and exploitation

In May 2020, the *New York Times* (of all media) first reported on the widespread exploitation of migrant children who had been released to adults by an overburdened and underfunded immigration system. A series of follow-up stories highlighted the bureaucratic negligence that led so many children to be placed at risk. The disturbing reports were generally ignored by other mainstream media outlets in light of the unproductive narrative. Nevertheless, a broken sponsor vetting process had allowed thousands of young children to be employed in dangerous workplaces (in clear violation of child labor laws) without consequence.

One can only imagine (recall the outrage over "children in cages") what media coverage would have been had the same circumstances occurred under a Trump administration.

THE BOTTOM LINE: January is "Human Trafficking Prevention Month" per presidential designation. But America's southern border has been left wide open during the Biden era. Make it make sense.

FAKE PAROLE

*[Parole decisions need only be] reasonable
and reasonably explained.*

—U.S. Supreme Court opinion
in *Biden vs. Texas*, 2022

The Biden administration's reversal of Trump-era border protections led to historic numbers of migrant encounters and gotaways. An avalanche of criticism followed, including from elected Democrats from towns and districts abutting the southern border. One response from Biden's DHS was to create new "programs" in order to manipulate/hide the real numbers from the general public.

A case in point was a trumpeted "parole program" that allowed 30,000 migrants a month from Cuba, Haiti, Nicaragua, and Venezuela to apply for permission to enter while still living in their home country. (Applicants were supposed to have U.S. sponsors who would support them financially.) When a significant drop in individuals from those countries showing up at the border occurred, the administration claimed success. Note: Twenty red states filed suit to challenge the legality of the shell game masquerading as the parole program.

A similar parole program applied to individuals from Colombia, El Salvador, Guatemala, and Honduras who had previously qualified for immigration (relatives of U.S. citizens and lawful permanent residents). Here, they were provided entry on a three-year pass. And the Biden-era practice of picking and choosing of favored—and disfavored—countries continued apace.

THE BOTTOM LINE: The concept of parole as used in the context of immigration law used to mean a case-by-case valuation of specific/special circumstances, but Biden administration borderless-ness has taken American immigration policy in a far different and dangerous direction.

THE PAROLE II (FLYING THE FRIENDLY SKIES)

These secretive flights have compounded the efforts of an already historic crisis at the Southern Border. We urge you to provide Congress and the American people with information as to where these illegal migrants have been deposited into the country and immediately terminate this practice.

—Letter from Rep. Russell Fry (R-SC) and twenty-two other GOP House Members to Troy Miller, Acting Commissioner of U.S. Customs and Border Protection

Another troubling aspect of Biden-era parole policy was to eliminate the long and often arduous walks to the border in favor of…airplane rides.

You read that right. An under-the-radar element of Mr. Biden's liberalized immigration parole program saw 320,000 migrants flown into forty-three U.S. airports in 2023 alone via the CBP One cell phone app, per a well-publicized report from Todd Bensman at the Center for Immigration Studies. The report noted that each individual would be eligible for a two-year renewable work authorization.

Think about this the next time you are put on hold while attempting to change a flight. You might reflect on what not so long ago was a *process* of immigration parole (typically limited to major crisis situations or case-by-case evaluations) has morphed into a frequent flyer program under cover of darkness and away from the prying eyes of upset taxpayers and conservative media.

THE BOTTOM LINE: Joe Biden's parole program is estimated to have brought in excess of a million parolees directly into the U.S., a vast and under-analyzed expansion of what had previously been a narrow program focused on egregious instances of human rights abuse.

FENTANYL

Fentanyl is the single deadliest drug threat our nation has ever encountered.

—DEA Administrator Anne
Milgram, August 19, 2022

My former deputy drug czar wife (under President Trump) will tell you how Chinese-manufactured fentanyl reached the U.S. through domestic mail delivery during the early days of the Trump administration. She will further tell you that Mr. Trump made it his business to tell Xi Jinping to stop it—which he did. (Note: On May 1, 2019, President Xi fulfilled his commitment to the G20 intergovernmental economic forum to formally control all forms of fentanyl as a class of drugs.) Importation accordingly decreased until a new Biden administration decided to open the southern border. A new era was thereby launched wherein fentanyl precursors are transported from China to labs in Mexico and then trafficked through ports of entry into the United States.

The resulting damage is easily measured. The CDC reports that 107,375 Americans died of drug overdose/poisoning from January 2021 to January 2022. Sixty-seven percent of those deaths were due to synthetic opioids such as fentanyl. The Drug Enforcement Administration reports that in 2022 it seized more than 379 million doses of fentanyl—enough to kill off the entire country. It makes one wonder how many doses got through our porous border.

THE BOTTOM LINE: You have to hand it to Xi Jinping and the CCP. The dictator and his political party are proving quite flexible in their ongoing mission to inflict death and destruction on America.

HORSE WHIPS

We know that those images painfully conjured up the worst elements of our nation's ongoing battle against systemic racism.

—DHS Secretary Alejandro Mayorkas repeating the false claim that his agents had whipped migrants despite knowing the story was false, September 24, 2021

Recall the mainstream media going nuclear after video footage emerged of Border Patrol agents on horseback allegedly using whips to control migrants seeking to cross the border at Del Rio, Texas. Here then was the perfect narrative: "racist" law enforcement utilizing brutal tactics against helpless asylum-seeking migrants. Democrats in Congress and immigration rights groups deplored the Border Patrol. Never to be out-demagogued, President Biden promised, "Those [agents] will pay." Similarly, the DHS secretary chipped in with the above-cited condemnation. Four days later, Mayorkas admitted he "made the statement without seeing the images."

And then…a nine-month investigation revealed that horse reins were not utilized during the "unprecedented surge" of approximately 15,000 Haitians at the International Bridge—but at least one agent had used "denigrating language" during the melee.

In the end, heaping helpings of (made-for-television) moral indignation were used up for one agent's use of inappropriate language during a tense border encounter. Per usual, there was no apology forthcoming from Capitol Hill or the White House press room.

THE BOTTOM LINE: Beware false reporting by the legacy media, especially when the alleged facts fit so nicely into a preexisting narrative.

DRESS-UPS

People are saying that if you are out on the streets the Border Patrol will get you and deport you because the president is

*coming to El Paso and they don't want
him to see the reality of things.*

—Maria Rodriguez, Venezuelan migrant
living in a dumpster in El Paso, Texas, on the
eve of President Biden's visit to the border, as
quoted in the *New York Post*, January 7, 2023

Remember the panicked response when your parents showed up unannounced at the front door to your college dorm? You immediately instructed your roommates to hold them off until your living space could be made at least minimally respectful. Such is the modus operandi the Border Patrol was required to follow when dignitaries visited the Biden-era southern border.

Per the *New York Post*, this was precisely the situation that preceded the president's only visit to the border—an early January 2023 quickie to El Paso, Texas, wherein local encampments were dismantled while hundreds of Mexican migrants were sent back across the border on the eve of the president's visit.

The agency's Inspector General found that the "dress-ups" were meant to create the illusion of preparedness for any forthcoming surge—and that post visit the scene would return to the status quo of overcrowding and general chaos. The IG further found that the Border Patrol and Immigration and Customs Enforcement were stretched beyond reason because the agencies had been level-funded despite their widely expanded scope of mission.

THE BOTTOM LINE: Feel bad for the professionals charged with protecting our borders when forced to participate in "dress-up" rituals for the political benefit of the Biden administration.

THE WALL I (THE BUILD)

*You, President Biden, you are the first president
of the United States in a very long time that
has not built even one meter of wall.*

—Mexican President Andrés Manuel
López Obrador, January 11, 2023

*The wall is in my view immoral, expensive,
unwise.… I don't think [the president]
said he was going to pass billions of
dollars of cost…on to the taxpayer.*

—Nancy Pelosi, April 23, 2017

No issue produces more truly dumb soundbites than "the Wall," as in the partially built edifice that represents the dividing line between our southern border and Mexico.

Speaker Pelosi's Democratic Party labeled the wall—most walls, in fact—"racist." Conversely, President Trump has called for the completion of a "big, beautiful" border wall since the very minute he rode down that escalator at Trump Tower.

Both sides of the divide enjoyed a degree of Trump-era success. For progressives, the noun morphed into a rallying cry against the GOP's alleged "nativist" instincts, while the president managed to complete 458 miles of border wall, though a significant portion was replacement rather than new construction (this despite a steady array of roadblocks from litigation-happy Democrats and environmental groups). Alas, everything came to a stop when Joe Biden assumed office and ordered a cessation to new construction.

Still, few were willing to state the inconvenient facts of border wall construction out loud: an extraordinarily long, diverse border means a physical wall in certain places, but other assets (fixed-wing aircraft, helicopters, drones, sensors, and Border Patrol) where more practical.

Addendum: As the manuscript for this book was nearly complete, a strange announcement took place in Washington, D.C.: Homeland Security Secretary Mayorkas announced an immediate need to "construct physical barriers" in response to recent armies of migrants rushing the border…after which he doubled down on the administration's opposition to a border wall.

THE BOTTOM LINE: You can expect more insultingly stupid (and confusing) immigration-related advertisements as election season approaches. The symbolism is just too juicy for the image makers to ignore. But it would benefit all involved to remembers that walls…work. It's why so many are built.

THE WALL II (SPARE PARTS)

[Border wall construction is a] waste of money that directs attention from genuine threats to our homeland security.

—President Joe Biden, Proclamation on the Termination of Emergency with Respect to the Southern Border of the United States and Redirection of Funds Directed to Border Wall Construction, January 20, 2021

In May 2023, Republican Sens. Roger Wicker (MS), Ted Cruz (TX), and Joni Ernst (IA) introduced the Finish It Act. The bill would require the federal government to utilize previously purchased steel structures in order to extend the U.S.-Mexico border wall or make the structures available for similar use by state governments. The sponsors noted that the Biden administration had been spending $47 million a year to store wall-related materials since Mr. Biden ordered the above-referenced stop to construction upon taking power.

In response, the administration began a sales campaign to sell off the panels before the GOP House could pass corresponding legislation. The online auction marketplace described the sales items as "excess border wall materials that the U.S. Army Corps of Engineers had turned over…for disposition and are now for sale." As expected, congressional Republicans screamed bloody murder, but the sales proceeded.

THE BOTTOM LINE: Cynical? Yes, Effective? You bet. Walls work, so of course the Biden administration would go about the business of making it more difficult to build one. It's just one more option taken away from a sane border control strategy.

THE WALL III (DIVERSION)

*Biden Administration spending big
to make ports of entry green while
trying to yank border wall funds.*

—Headline in the *Daily Caller*, March 14, 2024

Per the GAO (Government Accountability Office), the Biden administration took congressionally appropriated taxpayer funds intended for border wall construction and redirected them to a variety of environmental mitigation projects.

In effect, Mr. Biden and his cabinet secretaries worked together to repurpose construction funds (originally appropriated between fiscal year 2018 and fiscal year 2021) into a funding source for a variety of environmental initiatives, including eminent domain litigation and remediation efforts in venues where the wall already stood.

THE BOTTOM LINE: Here, yet another pillar of the Biden administration's southern border legacy: selling off previously purchased wall panels and redirecting wall-related construction funds all while inviting the world to our shores. The resulting misery and chaos is no surprise.

SANCTUARY CITIES

People are angry that a commonsense thing like securing the border or ending sanctuary cities is somehow considered extreme. It's not extreme; it's common sense. We need to secure the border.

—Carly Fiorina, former Hewlett-Packard CEO and presidential candidate, July 12, 2015

"Sanctuary cities" has become a phrase so familiar that we no longer pause to think about what it really means. All of which is a real-life problem because it means *some* cities (and states) have gone all in on their refusal to cooperate with federal immigration officials.

Here, progressive local administrations follow a pick-and-choose option of which federal office with which to cooperate—hardly a policy that engenders respect for the rule of law, but not such a problem for the open-border advocates within the Biden administration.

Still, even the most progressive of local politicians tends to curb his or her sanctuary enthusiasm when newly arriving migrants begin to overwhelm local resources, as was the case in the late summer and early fall of 2023. Seems even the "let 'em come" crowd has its limits when the dinner bill comes due—and actual citizens start giving them the "What for?" at town meetings.

An important aside: America's experience with the latest round of illegal migration reveals that the vast majority of migrants are not asylum seekers but rather economic refugees looking for a better life—an inconvenient, counter-narrative distinction too often buried in media reporting on the "Great Migration" of the Biden years.

THE BOTTOM LINE: When it comes to the great debate of Biden-era immigration policy, definitions count—especially where the safety and security of the American people are at issue.

DNA TESTING

The recent termination of DNA family testing by the Biden administration is a distressing decision that puts innocent lives at risk and undermines our commitment to combatting the heinous crimes of human trafficking and child exploitation.

—Jim Desmond, San Diego County
Supervisor, September 5, 2023

One devastating consequence of a porous southern border is the proliferation of human trafficking. A foolproof way to at least minimize the resulting damage is rapid DNA testing—a process that ensures children are the offspring of the alleged parents rather than the victims of child traffickers through use of a fake parent/mule.

Nevertheless, the Biden Department of Homeland Security terminated all such testing at the border on May 31, 2023, despite evidence reflecting that up to a third of tested children were unrelated to the alleged parents. (Whether the termination was related to the fifteen-month testing backlog on immigrants fourteen years of age or older—as reported by the Daily News Foundation—is anyone's guess.)

In response, on July 7, 2023, U.S. Sens. Cindy Hyde-Smith (R-MS) and Marsha Blackburn (R-TN) introduced legislation (End Child Trafficking Now Act) that would reintroduce DNA testing for migrant children.

THE BOTTOM LINE: This is how far an open-borders administration is willing to go: a new federal law must be passed in order to force the federal government to protect innocent children from sex traffickers.

FLOATING BARRIERS AND RAZOR WIRE

Texas will see you in court.

—Texas Gov. Greg Abbott upon learning
that the Department of Justice intended to
commence litigation over Texas's floating
barriers on the Rio Grande River, July 21, 2023

The federal government's unwillingness to protect the peace at our southern border led Texas Gov. Greg Abbott to install floating border barriers in the Rio Grande River near Eagle Pass, Texas, as part of his homemade border policy labeled "Operation Lone Star."

Despite the demonstrated success of Lone Star (394,000 apprehensions, 31,300 arrests, and 29,000 felony charges as of July 31, 2023), the Biden Justice Department responded in the usual way: "We're going to sue you." But the statutory grounds of the lawsuit (alleged violation of the federal Rivers and Harbors Act and lack of approval from the Army Corps of Engineers) was merely gloss for the government's near complete failure to enforce border security from the very first day of the Biden era.

A distressingly similar situation arose three months later when Governor Abbott was forced to sue the federal government to stop Border Patrol agents from cutting razor wire in order to allow *more* illegal migrant crossings along the Texas border—a practice that ended with an order from a U.S. district court judge (but which was subsequently overturned by the Supreme Court in January of 2024).

THE BOTTOM LINE: Governor Abbott's willingness to take matters into his own hands spoke to the frustration felt by Texas and other border states regarding the specter of more than eight million migrants appearing at their doorstep in response to Mr. Biden's open invitation to the world. There will certainly be more "floating bordergate" chapters to come as this test case winds its way through the courts.

PARALLEL UNIVERSE

This is nothing more than an attempt to siphon taxpayer money from law enforcement and hand it over to anti-enforcement activists.

—Jon Feere, former ICE Chief of Staff, as quoted in The Daily Caller, August 27, 2023

An unprecedented era of unlimited immigration may have been the Biden administration's intended goal, but the sudden impact of all those "new" Americans on local social services was a shock for red and blue state and local governments.

In response, the Biden administration decided to go lite on enforcement (of course) and heavy on expanded social services. And not just government-provided social services. Per progressives' go-to play, Biden's ICE solicited nonprofit participation in a new program entitled "Release and Reporting Management," an initiative that would utilize progressive-oriented activist groups to provide monitoring ("check-in") oversight and a wide variety of social welfare services (food, board, medical, transportation, education, and legal support) for illegal migrants.

The byproducts of such an approach are transparent: continue to separate ICE from its traditional enforcement role; continue to degrade resources intended for custodial detention; and create what amounts to a parallel welfare bureaucracy devoted to those who broke our immigration laws in the first place.

THE BOTTOM LINE: Open borders activists hate ICE as presently constituted. The goal is to slowly but surely transform the agency from an enforcement entity into

a social services provider, and all in plain sight. There
is no shortage of chutzpa within today's left.

SPACEX

*U.S. law requires at least a green card to be
hired at SpaceX, as rockets are considered
advanced weapons technology.*

—Elon Musk tweet, June 16, 2020

*SpaceX was told repeatedly that hiring
anyone who was not a permanent
resident of the United States would
violate international arms trafficking law,
which would be a criminal offense.*

—Elon Musk tweet, August 25, 2023

Elon Musk did the unthinkable. He switched "sides." And he
did it in spectacular fashion. Seems the serial entrepreneur and
onetime darling of the environmental left had become increasingly frustrated with progressive enthusiasm for speech control. And so he bought Twitter for $44 billion.

As a consequence, Musk exposed the cozy relationship between Biden's executive branch agencies and the
uber-progressive former CEO Jack Dorsey. He also welcomed Tucker Carlson and Mr. Trump on his platform. All of
which resulted in Musk finding himself in Biden AG Merrick
Garland's crosshairs.

How do we know this? Because the DOJ sued SpaceX in
August of 2023 *for failing to hire enough alien asylum seekers* in

violation of the Immigration and Nationality Act. You read that right. The government sued the Musk space entity because it (presumably) preferred to hire actual U.S. citizens and green-card holders rather than noncitizens without green cards in a highly sensitive workplace.

A separate media report noted that the Department of Justice was also looking into the "perks" Mr. Musk enjoyed pursuant to his leadership position at Tesla.

Alas, the combative Mr. Musk refused to roll over in the face of the Biden administration's intimidation tactics. He sued the government, pointing out that the sensitivity of next-generation technology was an essential element within America's national defense strategy.

THE BOTTOM LINE: Poke the multibillionaire bear—and you will get a lot more than you bargained for.

MISPLACED PRIORITIES

Who are the folks coming? Their names, their health records, have they been vaccinated for tuberculosis, varicella, or chicken pox? What are their employment skills? This is where the system has collapsed, [and] is a total disconnect between the federal government, the state government, the city of New York, and the 57 counties. It's a system in chaos right now.

—Stephen Acquario, Executive Director, New York Association of Counties, in Spectrum News, August 14, 2023

The "reimagining" (per the left's preferred verb) of ICE from immigration enforcement to social welfare agency was one step, but only one rung along the way in the Biden administration's campaign to create a distinct welfare program for recently arrived illegal migrants.

This was especially the case in the federal response to New York City Mayor Eric Adams (once a fan of sanctuary cities), who went off the reservation after the arrival of 100,000 migrants into NYC during the summer and fall of 2023. As the mayor's attempt to offload thousands of migrants to upstate New York towns and cities ran into stiff resistance (more than two dozen New York counties passed local rules barring hotels/motels from entering into contracts to house the migrants), the Biden administration came to the rescue with $100 million of work assistance on behalf of migrants who were employment eligible but had not applied for work authorizations.

It should be noted that thousands of migrants had previously secured jobs (and been able to forgo required asylum claim wait times) by utilizing the Biden administration's "CBP One app"—an application that provides immediate work authorization for illegals sponsored by the Department of Homeland Security.

So there you have it in a nutshell: Resources taken from a porous border lead to millions of mostly unskilled migrants sent to previously virtue signaling but wholly unprepared cities that in turn beg the people who caused the problem in the first place (the feds) to bail them out. And they do, with your money. And the immigration carousel continues to turn. And American citizens finish second again.

THE BOTTOM LINE: Seems the welfare of legal, taxpaying, hard-working American citizens is not a priority of the Biden administration. Only a national election will fix the problem.

A MURDER

I shouldn't have used "illegal." It's "undocumented"…I'm not going to treat any of these people with disrespect. They built this country.

—President Joe Biden, March 8, 2024

The president's fourth State of the Union speech was a partisan campaign call to arms focused on his party's progressive base. Indeed, the certain Republican nominee and former president (Trump) was a prime focus of Mr. Biden's "Let's save democracy" narrative.

But the horrific (and politically inconvenient) murder of college coed Laken Riley out for a jog in a suburban Atlanta neighborhood by an illegal migrant had captured the nation's attention on the eve of the big speech. For Republicans, the murder was seen as still more evidence of Mr. Biden's failed border policy that had led approximately ten million migrants to enter the U.S. over the previous thirty-eight months. A tense environment got even more tense when Congresswoman Marjorie Taylor Greene interrupted Mr. Biden mid-speech with a demand that he say her name—which he proceeded to do, albeit while mispronouncing it—"Laken," not "Lincoln."

Yet it was Mr. Biden's use of the term "illegal" when referring to the alleged murderer that upset progressives. The president's pitiful rejoinder/apology came the next day and is reflected above.

THE BOTTOM LINE: For much of the left, the use of a so-called pejorative—"illegal"—when referring to an alleged murderer was a serious faux pas. As if *correctly* referring to a migrant's immigration status was in any way relevant to the context of such a terrible incident.

RADIO SILENCE

That's a problem.

—Raul Ortiz, former head of U.S. Border
Patrol, on never having the opportunity to
discuss border issues with President Joe
Biden or Vice President Kamala Harris

During the 2020 campaign, candidate Joe Biden promised a more humane border policy that would end the "mean-spirited" reign of the xenophobic Trump era. After the election, President Biden in fact appointed Vice President Kamala Harris as his "Border Czar." All of this to create the impression the southern border would be a priority item for the Biden-Harris administration going forward.

History records the complete collapse of border control over the next four years despite often heated denials from Secretary of Homeland Security Alejandro Mayorkas and other members of the administration. Indeed, only on the eve of the 2024 campaign—and trailing badly in the polls—would the president acknowledge the continuing dysfunction at the border.

It was against this backdrop that Raul Ortiz, the former head of U.S. Border Patrol (and leader of twenty-one thousand border agents), charged that neither the president nor vice president had ever bothered to meet with him. And this at a time of unprecedented numbers of migrants crossing over into the U.S.

THE BOTTOM LINE: The two most powerful people in the world never took the time to meet the person who was in charge of *controlling* a continuously unfolding humanitarian disaster at America's southern border.

SUBSIDIES, INC.

More Americans are defaulting on their auto loans than at any point since the Great Depression. They won't be able to keep their cars just because they can't find work in the Biden economy. Meanwhile, foreigners don't have to worry about repaying their loans or even about driving—they can travel the sunny skies for free on your dime.

—Rep. Jim Banks (R-IN)

Just when you think Biden immigration policy has hit rock bottom…it gets worse.

How else to describe the State Department's funding of the International Organization for Migration's Travel Loan Program? This beauty gives refugees zero-interest, penalty-free "loans" that can be waived due to bankruptcy or unemployment—and the only sanction for default is a reduced credit score!

Note: In fiscal year 2023, close to $3 billion was appropriated for the Travel Loan Program.

THE BOTTOM LINE: That Biden executive agencies worked together to shepherd as many illegal migrants as possible into the U.S. is without doubt. That the plan unfolded against the backdrop of spiraling inflation and dramatic increases in the cost of living is equally without doubt. Here, as usual, "America First" has become "America (and American taxpayers) Last."

WALKAWAYS

*They're walkaways…What's driving 85
percent of this crisis is bad policy.*

—Mark Morgan, Former Chief Operating
Officer and Acting Commissioner of
U.S. Customs and Border Protection

Biden border policy is often so inept—so ludicrous—that it seems more parody than real life. Such is the case with a recently evolved category of illegally entering migrants—"walkaways."

Note that this particular newly hatched brand of illegal migrant is distinguished from "gotaways"—those who literally escape into the interior without arrest or detention. (Recently revised statistics place gotaways in the neighborhood of two million since 2021.)

Back to the more sedate walkaways. These are migrants who enter illegally—but then *wait* to be arrested. They often go undetected for days because Border Patrol is so overwhelmed with its new clerical duties. Accordingly, walkaways will do one of the following: reverse course back to Mexico (since they are not under arrest and have not been put through field interviews), walk into the country's interior (similar to the got-aways), or wait it out until Border Patrol finally has enough manpower to arrest and process them.

THE BOTTOM LINE: There is some legal uncertainty as to the obligation of Border Patrol to provide for medical/life necessities for the walkaways while they are *not* under detention. What *is* settled is how Biden border "policy" is dangerous to everyone impacted by the invasion of our southern border since 2021.

HOME SWEET HOME

You are not going to be able to commandeer someone's private property and expect to get away with it.

—Florida Governor Ron DeSantis on signing legislation ending squatters' rights in Florida

Yet another consequence of Mr. Biden's open borders is a squatters epidemic. Yes, the old problem of desperate homeless people breaking into abandoned dwellings simply to keep warm has morphed into illegal migrants raiding (and squatting in) private homes without the owner's knowledge and then using the legal system to extend their free stay.

The practice of mostly blue state legislatures and munici-palities giving property rights to squatters is beyond ludicrous. Here, the woke, no borders, "everyone is a citizen of the world" immigration dream comes full circle. Migrants are crossing over the border illegally, breaking into private residences, asserting their "right" to the property, and then proving difficult or impossible to remove under statutory legal protections that are too often laborious and expensive for the rightful owner to contest.

Think about this the next time you are contemplating an extended stay away from home.

THE BOTTOM LINE: The right to private property is simply one more basic freedom now in the crosshairs of those who seek to fundamentally transform the culture.

STRAIGHT FROM THE BOWELS OF HAMAS

Biden Reportedly Considering
Importing Gaza to America

—Headline in the *Daily Caller*, May 21, 2024

Just when the American people thought Biden-era immigration policy could not possibly get more dangerous…it did. Witness the above headline that greeted Americans during the very same week anti-Israel/pro-Hamas unrest was breaking out on U.S. campuses across the country.

Who else but the Biden administration could think it a good idea to bring thousands of people long indoctrinated into antisemitism and unfamiliar with Western/American values of pluralism, free speech, religious liberty, and constitutional Republicanism to the shores of a country suddenly shaken by those very same malignant teachings? Not to mention the still unknown number of terrorist sympathizers who had managed to sneak through Joe Biden's porous southern border over the past forty months.

Numerous commentators noted that Biden's gambit stood in stark contrast to surrounding Arab nations' well-established policy of resistance to large-scale immigration from Gaza.

THE BOTTOM LINE: The people of Palestine elected Hamas. Over 70 percent of Gazans believe the October 7, 2023 murderous rampage against innocent Israeli citizens was justified. And now Joe Biden thinks it a good idea to resettle those same people in the United States. Sublime.

CAMPUS CRIMINALS

[I]f people are "looking in the camera and saying, 'I am Hamas,' we should believe them" and add them to the terrorist watch list and no-fly list.

—Senator Marsha Blackburn (R-TN)

Foreign students are typically highly valued full tuition gold for American colleges and universities. The schools are accordingly hesitant to allow student entanglements (especially arrests) with the legal system, a policy widely followed during the anti-Israel demonstrations on American campuses during the late spring of 2024. And then, of course, there was Joe Biden's politically calculated measured response about all the unrest as aptly described in other chapters herein.

Both factors explain why Biden's Department of Homeland Security and Immigration and Customs Enforcement (ICE) were slow to move against foreign students who participated— sometimes violently so—in the college unrest.

Note that the problem children herein were not merely protesting Israeli government policy but more specifically advocating for (and engaging in) violent criminal behavior, including threats against Jewish students simply going about their campus business.

THE BOTTOM LINE: It should be clear: If you are a student here on a student visa and you violate our criminal laws, then you lose your right to be here. Full stop.

FROM BEIJING, WITH LOVE

The Biden administration gifted the Chinese intelligents an especially sparkling new policy...Why? To move them into the country even faster, including those who tossed their identity documents and might as well have given their names as Mickey Mouse.

—Todd Bensman, Senior National Security Fellow, Center for Immigration Studies

Xi Jinping and the Chinese Communist Party represent the greatest threat to stability in Southeast Asia, especially with respect to the regime's constant saber-rattling over Taiwan and artificial island construction projects in the South China Sea.

But Beijing is equally focused on replacing the U.S. as the world's dominant superpower. Witness the CCP's sophisticated spying operations—relentless efforts to steal American and Western intellectual property—and the "Belt and Road" initiative targeted at building infrastructure (and strategic alliances) in the developing world.

Against this disquieting backdrop comes news (first reported by the *Daily Caller*) of not only a serious spike in Chinese migrant encounters at the southern border (from 1,000 a year in the Trump years to 24,000 in 2023), but also of a dumbed-down vetting process specific to Chinese immigrants. Here the typical forty interview questions used in migrant interviews have been narrowed to a mere five (consisting of military service, education, place of birth, employment history, and political affiliation). Note that the influx of Chinese migrants exploded concurrent with the newly hatched, truncated interview process.

THE BOTTOM LINE: Experts who study migration patterns have speculated that Chinese intel officials are likely taking advantage of Biden's open border policy by sending operatives to not only infiltrate our country but also spy on Chinese nationals who have emigrated to America. Neither possibility appears to be of great concern to Mr. Biden's State Department or Department of Homeland Security.

CHAPTER 10

INSTITUTIONS

THE SENATE FILIBUSTER

> *Democrats want the American people to
> believe that the filibuster was not a Jim Crow
> relic in 2005, was not even a Jim Crow relic
> in 2020, just miraculously became a Jim
> Crow relic in 2021, just briefly stopped being
> a Jim Crow relic last Thursday, but it's now
> back to being a Jim Crow relic this week.*
>
> —Mitch McConnell (R-KY), Senate
> Majority Leader, January 18, 2020

The framers envisioned the filibuster as the ultimate safeguard for the legislative minority. Accordingly, the tactic has been employed by Republicans and Democrats alike from the earliest days of the republic. Indeed, the filibuster enjoyed the full support of Delaware Sen. Joe Biden for the vast majority of his thirty-six-year Senate career. To wit: when the GOP majority was considering suspension of the filibuster for federal judicial votes in 2005, it was none other than Joe Biden who labeled the move "a power grab" that "would eviscerate the Senate."

And then came the (coastal) progressive left and the need to transform the way our elected officials transact the nation's business—especially the transformation (read: elimination) of procedures from the founders' era focused on the rights of smaller, rural states. The new goal: Demonize the filibuster as a relic of segregation (label it "racist") and jettison it. In other words, make the termination of the filibuster just another weigh station along the supercharged progressive highway.

THE BOTTOM LINE: "Power grabs" that would "eviscerate the Senate" are…typically in the eye of the beholder.

D.C. STATEHOOD

*[The president] believes they
deserve representation, that's why
he supports D.C. statehood.*

—Jen Psaki, White House Press
Secretary, March 19, 2021

The Biden administration fully supported forty-three Senate Democrats in their quest to make Washington, D.C., America's fifty-first state. Cold political calculation was at work here as two brand-spanking-new progressive senators would assuredly follow (President Trump lost D.C. by 86 points in 2020), thereby providing the left the necessary margin to sustain a Senate majority over most election cycles.

But then there is the inconvenient matter of contravening the express intent of the framers. A separate federal district was their original intent, and they accordingly granted Congress exclusive jurisdiction over the District in "all cases whatsoever."

The periodic budgetary and public safety failures that follow limited home rule in the District would under normal circumstances cause reasonable folks to hit the pause button on the statehood movement, but not so much this generation of uber-progressive activists. Local dysfunction does not bother them. The recent explosion in violent crimes such as carjacking and armed robbery is unfortunate, but this too shall pass. They have bigger fish to fry.

THE BOTTOM LINE: The never-ending focus of the statehood movement is the prospect of two new U.S. senators, sure to be reliably progressive votes.

WALTER REED HOSPITAL

It is incomprehensible that essential pastoral care is taken away from the sick and the aged when it was so readily available.... I earnestly hope that this disdain for the sick will be remedied at once and their First Amendment rights will be respected.

—Timothy P. Broglio, Archbishop for the Military Services, USA, April 7, 2023

During Holy Week of 2023, the Biden administration (led by only the second Catholic ever to be elected president of the

United States) terminated Catholic pastoral care at Walter Reed National Military Medical Center. You read that right. One of the world's most famous military hospitals chose Holy Week to issue a "cease and desist" order to the Franciscans who had provided pastoral care to active-duty service members and veterans for nearly the past twenty years. It was also made clear that the new vendor would be a "secular defense contractor."

An immediate and forceful opposition to the order from Catholics and Republican members of Congress (led by Sen. Marco Rubio of Florida) caused the administration to reverse its decision. The Franciscan priests were shortly thereafter allowed to resume their humanitarian mission.

A one-day story. But another unforced error committed by a progressive administration intent on bringing a relentless culture war to *every* sector of American life.

THE BOTTOM LINE: Another gratuitous chapter in the culture war campaign to further secularize America.

CHAPTER 11

RACE

RE-SEGREGATION

*A 2019 report from the National Association
of Scholars identifies 125 colleges that
"segregate graduation ceremonies."*

—Campus Reform, April 20, 2023

The reality of resegregation on American college campuses is here and now. You read that correctly: some American colleges have turned back the clock of equality in order to segregate their dormitories and even graduation ceremonies in the name of equity.

Now sit back and ponder the specter of separate (and, I assume, equal) graduation ceremonies at some of America's most elite colleges and universities. And the fact that those very same institutions brag about their segregated events. And the fact that graduates are taught this type of segregation by race/ethnicity is appropriate. And that the Biden Department of Education has no problem with it at all. Then…think about

Dr. King's wonderful dream and try to fathom how the campaign for racial equality could have gone off the rails this badly.

THE BOTTOM LINE: The campaign to normalize resegregation on campus is a particularly obnoxious aspect of progressive indoctrination. People of goodwill—from all over the political spectrum—need to take it down as soon as possible.

BLACK FARMERS

It appears that in enacting Section 1005 Congress relies, albeit without any ill intention, on present discrimination to remedy past discrimination.

—U.S. District Judge Marcia Morales
Howard, June 23, 2021

Two things can be true at once. On the one hand, it is a terrible fact of history that segregation and Jim Crow exacted a terrible toll on African American farmers, many of whom continue to struggle to this day. Few would contest the government's interest in remedial assistance for this historically powerless group.

It is equally difficult to justify a race-based Covid relief program that denies federal aid to poor white farmers and ranchers on the basis of race alone. But that is precisely what the Biden administration attempted to do within the $1.9 billion stimulus package Congress passed in March 2021. That is, until a federal judge in Florida held such disparate treatment violated equal protection and shut the initiative down.

THE BOTTOM LINE: Need-based help for economically deprived victims of man-made disasters (segregation/discrimination)

and natural disasters (pandemics/hurricanes) is not divisive and brings similarly situated victims together. And all without the needless animosity produced by race politics.

HURRICANE IAN

[Ian relief will prioritize]…communities of color.

—Vice President Kamala Harris in the
aftermath of Hurricane Ian, October 1, 2021

In late September 2021, Hurricane Ian, an enormous tropical cyclone, slammed into the west coast of Florida near Cayo Costa Island. The storm killed 160 people (149 Floridians) and caused in the neighborhood of $50 billion to $60 billion in property damage.

On October 1, Vice President Harris offered the above-cited quote as Biden administration relief guidance. It was a policy neither she nor the president shied away from in the face of a torrent of criticism.

Nevertheless, the State of Florida's rapid response director attempted to quell brewing anxiety by assuring all Floridians that state aid would be a function of need "regardless of race or background."

That such a statement had to be issued *in 2023* speaks to how cynical race messaging is these days. But we now live in the delusory world of Biden-Harris, where *every* issue is viewed through a racial prism—even the fifth most powerful hurricane to ever hit the contiguous U.S.

THE BOTTOM LINE: It was fortunate that such an insidious comment was immediately shot down by state officials,

but the statement reflects a cringeworthy preoccupation with race that leaves Americans bitter and divided.

PHILADELPHIA

The most dangerous terrorist threat to our homeland is white supremacy. And I'm not saying this because I'm at a Black HBCU. I say it wherever I go.

—President Joe Biden, commencement address at Howard University, May 13, 2023

The folksy monikers were everywhere during the 2020 campaign: "Amtrak Joe." "Grandfather Joe." The middle-class man of "moderate temperament." A lifelong politician who could bring America together again after a hyper-polarized Trump era. It all sounded so promising—when you said it real fast…or failed to read between the lines…or neglected to notice Biden's own fiery race rhetoric on the campaign trail.

But the political opening represented by the January 6 "insurrection," and the need to redirect public attention away from repeated domestic and foreign policy failures, necessitated a turn to the progressive left's go-to play—the race card. And so just about every Biden policy address thereafter (most spectacularly the daunting blood-red background featuring U.S. Marine guards stationed in front of Independence Hall in Philadelphia on September 1, 2022) bemoaned the rise of a newly empowered alt-right determined to wage a race war—to put African Americans "back in chains," to borrow a phrase from a previous Biden speech.

The good news is that such rhetoric never matched the facts on the ground, despite repeated administration attempts to associate America's armed forces and police departments with breeding grounds for "white supremacy." The bad news was that the mainstream media—as usual—indulged the ever-escalating narrative. Polarizing? Sure. Ugly? You bet. Effective? Always.

THE BOTTOM LINE: At some point, the race card has to run its course. But we are not there yet. We know this because the card continues to be played—and keeps working— even though more people seem to be wising up to it.

MILITARY PROMOTIONS

The [Biden] administration strongly opposes the House's sweeping attempts to eliminate the [Defense Department's] long-standing DEIA efforts and related initiatives to promote a cohesive and inclusive force.

—Biden Office of Management
and Budget, July 2023

What we're trying to do is move to a color-blind, race-neutral worldview, where we're focused on building a national defense and a military that is focused on, you know, blowing things up and killing people, not on social engineering wrapped in a uniform.

—U.S. Rep. Chip Roy (R-TX) as quoted
in the *New York Post*, July 11, 2023

The Defense Appropriations Bill for Fiscal Year 2024 contained a Republican-sponsored provision that required all promotion decisions to be based on merit alone—the best person for the job, so to speak.

The casual observer in 2023 might think such a provision superfluous—that military promotions are of course all about the ability to lead soldiers while in harm's way because the U.S. military has "Job One" when it comes to protecting our democracy. But this is the Biden era, where even battlefield performance is judged through a woke prism. Here, another example of merit relegated to the bleachers in favor of diversity, equity, inclusion, and (now) accessibility considerations.

THE BOTTOM LINE: Somewhere in Beijing, Xi Jinping and his henchmen are laughing at us (again).

FLORIDA SCHOOLS

It is the case that Africans proved resourceful, resilient, and adaptive, and were able to develop skills and aptitudes which served to their benefit, both while enslaved and after enslaved…. It was never said that slavery was beneficial to Africans.

—Dr. William B. Allen, author and educator, on the work of Florida's African American History Standards Workgroup, July 2023

Put yourself in Kamala Harris's place for a moment. You have artfully weaponized race on more than one occasion (most famously on that debate stage against Joe Biden during the 2020 campaign). You are now facing the fight of your life against one of two likely GOP candidates, and one had the temerity to empower a group of African American scholars to write an objective new black history curriculum for Florida schools. One that includes lessons about how some enslaved people learned specialized trades while in bondage, which they utilized to better their lives when freed—a defying-the-odds, against-all-expectations positive moral for young people, but one that a true-blue progressive just cannot allow to stand. What to do?

Well…you do what you always do. You trek to Florida, unleash a tirade on the new teaching guide ([an] "attempt to teach that enslaved people benefited from slavery"), and then you leave. Woke message delivered. Fawning media coverage assured. No fuss, no muss. Except that the esteemed chairman of Florida's African American History Standards Workgroup then takes you down with the above quote.

THE BOTTOM LINE: Gaslighting serious scholars on important issues is dangerous and generally ineffective as a political tactic.

CHAPTER 12

SPEECH

DISINFORMATION CZAR

Information laundering is really quite ferocious.

*It's when a huckster takes some lies and
makes them sound precocious,\by saying
them in Congress or a mainstream outlet,\so
disinformation's origins are slightly less atrocious.*

—Nina Jankowicz, TikTok video
sung to the *Mary Poppins* tune
"Supercalifragilisticexpialidocious"

On April 27, 2022, the Biden Department of Homeland Security announced the formation of the first-ever Disinformation Governance Board. The new panel's charter was to "coordinate countering misinformation related to Homeland Security." President Biden named a thirty-three-year-old woman, Nina Jankowicz, as Executive Director. Jankowicz was selected due to her supposed expertise in the field of "disinformation research." And yes, it appears that really is a new academic discipline.

The formation of the information-gathering entity raised immediate concerns on the right and among civil libertarians, but it was a truly nutty TikTok video wherein the new czar mimicked a popular *Mary Poppins* tune while singing about the need for her new position that got everyone's attention. The goofy rendition played to poor reviews as the newly labeled "Bureau of Truth" rapidly became batting-practice fodder for Republican critics around the country. To make matters worse, it was subsequently revealed that Jankowicz had been in the vanguard of the influencers and partisan hacks who had cast doubt on the legitimacy of Hunter Biden's laptop from hell.

Alas, this latest and not-so-greatest exercise in government censorship came crashing down when Jankowicz resigned and the administration "paused" the new panel. One can only speculate how much fun a new Republican House would have had with this truly terrible operation.

THE BOTTOM LINE: Here, government regulation of free speech had (almost) advanced yet another step closer to Oceania, Big Brother, and the Ministry of Truth. If you do not recognize those entities, we are in more trouble than I thought.

WHAT IS A WOMAN?

An adult female person, a grown-up female person, as distinguished from a man or a child; sometimes, any female person.

—Webster's definition of "woman"

It had to occur at some point. And it indeed did occur at the most inopportune time for Biden-appointed Supreme Court nominee Ketanji Brown Jackson.

The scene was Judge Jackson's confirmation hearing before the Senate Judiciary Committee. The high court's first African American female nominee (and magna cum laude graduate of Harvard) was proceeding through the committee's questions in good order when (in hour thirteen) the senior senator from Tennessee was recognized. Sen. Marsha Blackburn asked the judge what not so long ago would have been a silly but easy-to-answer question: "Can you provide a definition for the word 'woman'?" Judge Jackson's reply: "I can't…not in this context. I'm not a biologist."

Such is all anybody needs to know about the impact—and progress—of progressive orthodoxy on American culture. Despite an earnest attempt to create context for her inability to answer (the definition was being "hotly discussed" and could come up in future court decisions), a cultural inflection point had been reached. In 2023 America, at least some public figures were afraid to define gender, even the "safe" chromosomal answer. And the president of the United States had no problem with it. And the media moved on to the next story.

THE BOTTOM LINE: Woke culture can make us unserious at the most inopportune moments.

DHS TERRORISM BULLETINS

[The Biden administration works to]
counter the influence and impact of

dangerous conspiracy theories that can
provide a gateway to terrorist violence.

—From Biden national security
team's statement on "disinformation"
and "misinformation" in response to
the president's first-day directive to
confront domestic terrorism, 2021

Commencing in January 2021, the Biden administration's Department of Homeland Security began issuing periodic terrorism threat advisory bulletins reflecting a "heightened threat environment inclusive of misinformation introduced and/or amplified by foreign and domestic threat actors." In February 2022, DHS issued a fifth such bulletin regarding "the proliferation of fake or misleading narratives aimed at "sow[ing] discord and undermin[ing] public trust in government institutions…which could potentially inspire acts of violence." We can safely assume that despite considerable objective evidence to the contrary, Trump-Russian collusion, the true origin of Covid-19, the efficacy of masks during a pandemic, and the authenticity of Hunter's laptop were the types of "fake" or "misleading" narratives the Biden administration was so concerned about. Still, everyone understood such notices were simply a part of the administration's ever-expanding initiative to combat "violent extremists" in the heartland in the aftermath of the January 6 attacks on the Capitol.

THE BOTTOM LINE: For the ascendant rhetoricians on the political left, no attempt to circumvent First Amendment rights can fall outside the ever-convenient January 6 narrative. As if lefty pundits within the mainstream media need more help.

SURVEILLANCE TRAINING

If liberty means anything at all, it means the
right to tell people what they do not want to hear.

—George Orwell

The headline says it all: "Biden Administration Launches Initiative to Train Public How to Spot Radical Conservatives and Fight Domestic Terrorism." Here, the Department of Homeland Security—ostensibly charged with protecting the homeland—is the lead agency charged with helping neighbors identify other neighbors who allegedly show signs of radicalization that could lead to terrorism.

Herein is yet another initiative predicated on the existence of a so-called "white supremacist movement" that has never been shown to possess large numbers of adherents, and issued around the time several FBI whistleblowers had come forward to allege politicized case reporting (including manipulation of investigative targets and supporting data) during the Biden era.

Many on the right (but not solely on the right) questioned the need for another political domestic security program on the prowl for citizens with conservative/traditional values, possibly including traditional Catholics, pro-lifers, free-speech advocates, anti-trans activists, and so-called election deniers from 2020.

THE BOTTOM LINE: If you still need a definition of inappropriate weaponization of government agencies during the Biden era...well, here it is.

SUPPRESSION, INC.

*During the Covid-19 pandemic, a period
perhaps best characterized by widespread
doubt and uncertainty, the United States
government seems to have assumed a role
similar to an Orwellian "Ministry of Truth."*

—U.S. District Judge Terry Doughty
in *Missouri vs. Biden*, July 4, 2023

The Biden era marshaled in a toxic marriage of government agencies and social media platforms, with a mutual goal to suppress disfavored opinion on issues ranging from the true origin of Covid to Hunter Biden's business dealings. The relationship blossomed as social media censored, shadow banned, and outright canceled content, all according to the dictates of the FBI, CDC, DOJ, DHS, and surgeon general, among others.

This "new normal" remained intact until the Trump-appointed Judge Doughty disbanded the disinformation all-star team on Independence Day 2023.

It was on that date Judge Doughty granted an injunction in *Missouri vs. Biden*, a case brought by the attorneys general of Missouri and Louisiana in order to block the above-cited government agencies from coordinating with social media platforms to chill critical speech. The opinion was a master class on the dangers and easily foreseen consequences of government content control.

The Biden administration noted an immediate appeal to the Fifth Circuit, a court dominated by Trump-appointed judges. Shortly thereafter, a three-judge panel of the court upheld the injunction, concluding that "the harms that radiate from such conduct extend far beyond just the plaintiffs; it impacts every social-media user." The full court subsequently upheld the injunction with respect to DHS (adding the Cyber and Infrastructure Security Agency), the White House, the surgeon general, the Centers for Disease Control, and the FBI.

THE BOTTOM LINE: The U.S. Supreme Court—where government-inspired influence schemes tend to meet their demise—agreed in October 2023 to hear *Missouri vs. Biden* during its 2023-24 term.

A POLITICAL INDICTMENT

Here is ten straight minutes of
Democrats denying election results.

—Republican National Committee research,
tweet, and video, September 4, 2022

Of the four prosecutions targeting President Trump, two emanated from Special Counsel Jack Smith. Note the title: Special counsels perform their work when the Department of Justice perceives a possible conflict of interest. They do not operate under daily department supervision but still must conform to DOJ regulations and procedures. This title is distinguished from independent counsels that did their work outside normal channels and, incidentally, without outside interference (at least to the time the independent counsel statute was allowed to expire in 1999).

Smith secured his second indictment from a grand jury in Florida after initiating a grand jury in Washington, D.C. The four counts alleged that the president's language challenging the 2020 election result constituted a conspiracy to commit fraud against the United States. In order to reach his burden of proof, Smith would be required to prove that Mr. Trump subjectively *knew* he lost the election but nevertheless proceeded to (repeatedly) proclaim otherwise. In other words, Trump lacked the freedom to state even inaccurate opinions about the "stolen" and "rigged" election—and (presumably) was somehow required to solely follow the advice of those who believed the result correct.

THE BOTTOM LINE: The freedom to challenge a political contest has not been particularly controversial in recent times. As reflected above, Democrats inside and outside of Congress contested GOP Electoral College slates in 2000, 2004, and most recently (how ironic) in 2016. Nobody thought to challenge *their* free speech rights to contest a national election. But this is the Biden era, and free speech is in the government's crosshairs. All bets are off. The kitchen sink is available. Trump must lose. Challenging times indeed.

U.S. WOMEN'S SOCCER TEAM

You've made your country proud.
Congratulations on an incredible run.

—President Joe Biden in the aftermath
of the U.S. women's national soccer
team's upset loss to Sweden in the
2023 World Cup, August 6, 2023

For the better part of two decades, the U.S. women's national soccer team enjoyed a dominant run on the world stage. That is, until an August 6, 2023, upset loss to Sweden ended the dynasty. It was the worst finish for the American squad in World Cup history. But the American public's usual love affair with a player or team with "America" emblazoned across their jerseys was decidedly missing after a majority of Team America refused to sing the national anthem or place a hand over their heart before the opening match against Vietnam. It was accordingly unsurprising that so many negative social media posts appeared in the hours after the defeat, with the sporting aspect of the tournament more a sideshow than the politics of it all.

Truth be told, much of Middle America had already tuned out, rejecting an emotional investment in a group of players whose public face was the outspoken purple-haired progressive Megan Rapinoe.

Never one to miss an opportunity to virtue signal, Joe Biden tweeted how proud he was of the team for its "spirit and determination—on *and off the field*." The not-too-subtle message was a rebuttal to large segments of the public that expect at least a modicum of patriotism from those who represent the country in international events.

THE BOTTOM LINE: The public image of the U.S. women's national soccer team took a hit that could linger for years. But one wonders whether the majority of the players care about their public image.

CISA

In the year since its creation…CISA metastasized into the nerve center of the federal government's domestic surveillance and censorship operations on social media.

—Interim Staff Report, House Committee on the Judiciary, Select Subcommittee on the Weaponization of the Federal Government, June 26, 2023

It is no easy task to keep up with the variety of Biden-era censorship operations. Lack of transparency is the primary obstacle, and never more so than with the case of the Cyber and Infrastructure Security Agency within the Department of Homeland Security.

This beauty was originally tasked with protecting America's critical infrastructure against foreign cyber threats but soon morphed into a domestic collection agency wherein CISA would notify social media platforms and/or *law enforcement agencies* whenever unapproved election-related "disinformation" was located (this according to the DHS Office of Inspector General). And once sued (and thereby exposed) in federal court, it morphed again into a nonprofit, the Elections Infrastructure Information Sharing and Analysis Center (EI-ISAC), heavily funded by federal tax dollars and assigned the task of becoming a "single point of reporting and tracking of misinformation across all channels and platforms." In essence, a one-stop speech suppression shop that "leverage[d] CISA's relationships with social media platforms." Note that while the Twitter Files and other testimonies reflect how uncomfortable (some) social media entities were with the heavy hand of government interference…they nevertheless typically indulged the government censors.

THE BOTTOM LINE: It appears that no amount of court injunctions or Musk-led exposés will dissuade the Biden administration from seeking to censor public expression that contravenes the official narrative.

FISH STORIES

Whatever his intentions, whether it's, you know, foggy memory about stuff that's going on decades ago or deliberate embellishment, this is an unfortunate pattern that keeps coming up again and again with Joe Biden.

—Daniel Dale, CNN fact checker,
September 12, 2023

First, what we are not talking about: spinnable yarns that are untrue (illegal immigration is seasonal; the inflationary spike will be temporary) but typical political overreach utilized in the wild, wild west of politics and campaigns by politicians of both parties.

What we *are* talking about are provably false statements—some serious, some silly—that constitute a pattern of problematic behavior over a period of decades. Note that every entry below has been widely reported in the legacy media, each is easily accessible by anyone so interested, and many predate the more cognitively limited Joe Biden of recent years.

A partial history of oft-repeated—and oft-reported—Biden untruths deserving of four Pinocchios:

- He was not opposed to the war in Afghanistan from the beginning;

- He has not cut the public debt in half;

- He did not visit Ground Zero on 9/12;

- He never funded 70,000 new major construction projects;

- He never drove a tractor trailer for a living;

- He never traveled 17,000 miles with Xi Jinping;

- He was never arrested at a civil rights rally;

- He never met Nelson Mandela as a young man;

- He did not attend civil rights organizing meetings in Wilmington, Delaware;

- He did not attend law school on a full scholarship;

- He did not graduate in the top half of his law school class;

- He was never asked by Golda Meir to act as an intermediary with Egypt during the Six Day War;

- He has never been in and out of Iraq and Afghanistan over forty times;

- His first wife and daughter were killed in a traffic accident—but not by a drunk driver;

- He never had a conversation about his travel miles (as vice president) with an Amtrak conductor named Angelo Negri;

- He has never declared a national climate emergency;

- He never gave his uncle a Purple Heart for serving in World War II;

- He never taught a political theory course at the University of Pennsylvania;

- His son Beau Biden died from cancer—not a service-related loss;

- His grandfather did not die a few days before he was born—and not in the same hospital;

- Al-Qaeda is not gone from Afghanistan.

THE BOTTOM LINE: Fish stories grow rotten when repeated and embellished.

EMPTY WARNINGS

There is no question that today's Republican Party is driven and intimidated by MAGA Republican extremists.

—President Joe Biden, September 28, 2023

Political theatrics and fearmongering over threats real and imagined, existential and newly emerging, dominated the Biden administration's communications strategy. On the domestic front, plenty of time and attention was devoted to high-profile admonitions/warnings concerning a wide variety of threats, ranging from "climate change" to "white supremacy" to rowdy parents at school board meetings to the eighteenth-century MAGA types said to possess rigid values on sex and gender.

Overheated rhetoric extended to foreign policy as well, as the public was constantly told that only an open-ended commitment to Ukraine would guarantee the long-term safety of Europe—and America. In the Middle East, America's reliable ally Israel was repeatedly warned about West Bank expansion, told to stand down in Gaza in the aftermath of the Hamas terror incursion of October 7, 2023, and then told to abide by a "two state solution" with the same people who have been at war with Israel since the founding of the Jewish state. And then, in the immediate aftermath of Hamas's bloody invasion from Gaza and a disquieting outbreak of antisemitism in the West—the vice president announced America's first "National Strategy to Counter Islamophobia."

THE BOTTOM LINE: The Biden administration issued countless, very public warnings about its favorite political targets—especially anything and everything associated with Make America Great Again. Yet far fewer warnings were issued regarding the Mexican drug cartels, illegal migrants, Xi Jinping, the mullahs in Tehran, or those seeking to loot and burn our inner cities.

AN EASTER SURPRISE

Is it really possible that no one in the Biden White House knew March 31st was Easter?

*Or are they so aggressively pro-transgender
that they wanted to insult Christians?*

—Newt Gingrich, Former Speaker of the House

The *secular* aspect of secular progressivism is often overlooked. One reason is that conservatives—particularly conservative Christians—have become acclimated to the daily insults and batterings by America's secular power centers, especially a mainstream media that regularly portrays religious conviction as bigoted and intolerant. But leave it to the Biden administration to go beyond the pale.

A spectacular (if delusory) case in point was the president's declaration that Easter Sunday 2024 would be known as "Transgender Day of Visibility." The announcement reached the public along with reports that Easter egg decorations at the White House would contain "no religious imagery." It was a "twofer" for the ages.

THE BOTTOM LINE: Substantially less people would have opined or even known about the presidential declaration had it been delivered the following Monday. But this administration could not resist the shock value. And this it certainly accomplished.

MORE FISH STORIES

An elderly man with a poor memory.

—Special Counsel Robert Hur's description
of Joe Biden, contained in a 388-page report
on Biden's retention of classified documents

- His uncle, Ambrose Finnegan, was not eaten by cannibals in New Guinea during World War II…but was killed in an aircraft crash off the coast of New Guinea.

- He did not ride in a train on the Francis Scott Key Bridge over the Patapsco River.

- He was never arrested as a child while standing on an African American family's porch during a protest against segregation.

- He was not the runner-up in state scoring during his high school football days.

- He did show classified information to a ghost-writer for his 2017 memoir.

- He has made more than $400,000 a year (including $11 million in 2011).

- Inflation was 1.4 percent when he took office, not 9 percent.

- He did not create fifteen million new jobs as president.

THE BOTTOM LINE: Fifteen lies in seventeen minutes per CNN during a May 8, 2024 interview *must* be some kind of a record.

MORAL CLARITY

You have enemies? Good. That means you've stood up for something, sometime in your life.

—Winston Churchill, Former
Prime Minister of the UK

"Moral clarity" is the leadership quality most often needed whenever circumstances require a leader to call out evil. Examples abound, but Americans commonly recognize Abraham Lincoln's "A house divided cannot stand" admonition regarding the immorality of slavery; Ronald Reagan's "Mr. Gorbachev, tear down this wall" demand in the face of Soviet repression in East Germany; FDR's "A day that will live in infamy" call to arms in the aftermath of Pearl Harbor; and Dr. Martin Luther King's "I have a dream" plea to a racially segregated America.

Alas, there were no such memorable words or phrases from Joe Biden in the aftermath of often violent anti-Israel/anti-Zionist/pro-Hamas riots at dozens of America's most elite colleges and universities in the late spring of 2024. Instead, the White House press operation (and especially Vice President Kamala Harris) ground out the usual criticisms of antisemitism and anti-Muslim rhetoric—as though there existed evidence of an equal threat from each side.

THE BOTTOM LINE: The Biden administration's often tepid response to leftist violence and anti-Jewish rhetoric on campus was sad but unsurprising in light of Biden's need to: (1) maintain the theme of "white supremacy" as the gravest threat to America and (2) stay in the weak and wobbly middle between Michigan's large Muslim Democrat voting bloc and traditional left-leaning Jewish Democrats caught off guard by rising anti-Zionist sentiment in the U.S.

A DEBATE DEBACLE

Washington is now full of surprises.
It is a city of people who display that practiced
faux shock. It is a city of Claude Rains…

—Jonathan Turley (in response to the
famous gambling scene from *Casablanca*)

The wildly anticipated first debate of the 2024 presidential cycle contained few substantive surprises: the voters were already well aware that the respective candidates possess vastly conflicting views regarding the issues of the day. But it was the sleepy, detached performance from the sitting president that made headlines—and made already worried Democrats even more desperate to find a possible replacement prior to the Democratic Convention in mid-August.

Still, what was a dreadful night for the incumbent was an even worse night for a legacy media that had been active players in the cover-up of Mr. Biden's deteriorating mental condition for years. Indeed, the scope of the media's willful negligence was laid bare to the entire country – and with only one hundred twenty-eight days to go until Election Day.

On the right, it was open season on Biden and the media (excuse the redundancy) as the universe of conservative pundits ridiculed the opposition for the phony narratives ("deepfakes") that had been used to cover for the president's clearly declining mental acuity. (Professor Jonathan Turley's above quote being one of the very best indictments).

THE BOTTOM LINE: The former senator and vice president had been a willing and useful vessel for the "beat Trump at any cost" Democrats until…he wasn't.

CHAPTER 13

VOTING RIGHTS

PHOTO ID

> *There is an unfolding assault taking place in*
> *America today—an attempt to suppress and*
> *subvert the right to vote in fair and free elections.*

—President Joe Biden, July 13, 2021

Probably *the* most frustrating issue to arise since the advent of woke-inspired cultural values concerns the appropriateness of requiring photo identification in order to vote. Somehow, this formerly innocuous requirement has morphed into demonized kindling material for practitioners of race politics. I should know. Providing public support for this common-sense requirement in a blue state is a tough sell in our present race-fueled environment.

For years, my go-to rationale was to impeach the credibility of the opposition, to stress how insensitive (and wrong) it was to insist that minorities are incapable of procuring some sort of self-identification when *everybody* requires some proof of identity in order to function in today's world. Alas, my go-to was repeatedly shot down by liberals outraged by my alleged "insensitivity."

After one too many confrontations with those who see all sorts of nefarious voting rights restrictions in voter affirmation, I hit upon a perfect analogy to make my case—or so I thought.

For me, springtime brings ragweed and sneezing fits, which means periodic visits to the pharmacy in order to buy Claritin-D—a process that requires production of my driver's license. That I have been a public figure in Maryland for many years is irrelevant. It is either produce a photo ID or forgo the purchase and literally suffer the consequences. My takeaway: If it's copasetic to require photo evidence of my identity in order to purchase seasonal allergy medicine, what's the big deal about the same requirement in order to exercise the most sacred right we have as Americans?

THE BOTTOM LINE: Few minds were actually changed by my good-faith efforts *or* the growing body of evidence that shows states with photo ID requirements see an *increase* in minority voting participation. And so the "photo ID is racist" narrative—led by an all too compliant President Joe Biden—continues to live and thrive within blue America.

NONCITIZENS

[Noncitizen voting in D.C.] will only
exacerbate the ongoing border crisis,
silence the voices of American citizens, and

open the door for foreign adversaries to
peddle influence in our nation's capital.

—U.S. Rep. James R. Comer
(R-KY), January 12, 2023

Noncitizen voting is barred in all federal elections and has not been allowed in state elections for about a century. But lately voting rights for noncitizens has picked up momentum in deep-blue venues, including New York City (subsequently struck down in the courts as unconstitutional) and in D.C., where the Biden administration opposed a vote of disapproval of D.C. noncitizen voting rights in the GOP-controlled House of Representatives.

One need not be a legal scholar to understand the dangers inherent in this movement, especially in light of the flood of illegal migrants that have crossed over our southern border during the Biden era. As with so many similar attempted disruptions of our cultural order, progressivism believes it occupies the moral high ground of voting rights, *even where the beneficiaries have gained illegal entry into the country.* In the words of U.S. Sen. Kirsten Gillibrand (D-NY), "There is no such thing as an illegal human"—a logical takeaway being that immigration law is superfluous in a world where no one is illegal.

THE BOTTOM LINE: One would think voting rights limited to actual citizens would constitute a real-world bright line. But nothing is quite so bright in Joe Biden's progressive universe.

GEORGIA AND THE ALL-STAR GAME

*[Georgia's election reform law is] Jim Crow
in the twenty-first century. It must end.*

—President Joe Biden, March 26, 2021

Fans are intimately familiar with how Biden-approved race rhetoric and virtue signaling have impacted professional sports—especially the NBA and NFL. But such misapplied virtue was taken to new heights in 2021 after Georgia Gov. Brian Kemp signed an election integrity measure strongly opposed by progressives. The amped-up race rhetoric that followed led Major League Baseball to move the annual All-Star Game from Atlanta to Colorado, citing the alleged "voter suppression statute" as the reason.

One wonders whether anyone connected to MLB took the time to read the statute. The Georgia bill broke no new ground and in fact contained familiar and commonsense reforms, including new identification requirements for requesting mail-in ballots and a shortened early voting period for runoff elections. To boot, the first Georgia election cycle under the new law (in 2022) saw historic African American turnout— just as the sponsors had predicted. But Atlanta had lost the opportunity to honor the recently passed Hank Aaron and to enjoy the tens of millions of dollars typically generated by the big game.[1]

---

[1]　On November 16, 2023, Major League Commissioner Rob Manfred announced that Atlanta had been selected for the 2025 Midsummer Classic. There was no mention of those allegedly controversial Georgia election reforms that remain on the books.

THE BOTTOM LINE: Nobody from MLB has anything to say about the Atlanta-based minority businesses that would have profited from the All-Star Game. Just another example of how woke leads to broke in the real world.

FEDERALIZATION

Democrats are poised to pass #HR-1, the #ForThePeopleAct, a historic reform package to restore the promise of our nation's democracy, defund the #CultureOfCorruption in Washington, and reduce the role of money in politics.

—Tweet from former House Speaker
Nancy Pelosi, March 8, 2019

It is no secret that Democrats far outpace Republicans when it comes to new-era Get Out the Vote (GOTV) strategies. This advantage was especially pronounced during Covid, wherein Democratic field organizers leveraged mail-in and vote harvesting techniques to outperform the GOP election day turnout advantage. This strategy allowed Joe Biden to follow a "stay in my basement" campaign while racking up in excess of eighty million votes in 2020. It also gave rise to a new and accurate criticism: "Republicans run campaigns; Democrats run elections."

But even this turnout advantage is not enough to guarantee a permanent Democrat majority. This fact of life led Joe Biden and progressive Democrats to attempt an electoral end run in the form of the highly trumpeted H.R. 1 in the 117th Congress.

The wish list of progressive initiatives contained therein would have federalized just about every aspect of our voting rights, including automatic voter registration, full felon voting rights restoration, expanded mail and early voting schedules, prohibition of voter roll purges, greater disclosure of "special interests," mandated independent redistricting commissions, prohibition of "discriminatory voter ID laws," and made election day a federal holiday, to name a few.

Fortunately, this federal (partisan) power grab could not pass even a Democratic-controlled Senate as the bill fell far short of the sixty votes needed to invoke cloture in the Senate. A close call—but a reminder that woke recognizes no bounds (especially federalism) in the pursuit of raw power.

THE BOTTOM LINE: You can bet the next iteration of H.R. 1 is on the shelf of some left-wing think tank, waiting for the day a progressive supermajority can fully bypass all those bothersome state election laws.

CHAPTER 14

WEAPONIZATION

THE FIFTY-ONE

*[The Hunter Biden laptop story had]
all the classic earmarks of a Russian
disinformation operation.*

—Statement contained in a public letter
signed by fifty-one former intelligence
officers concerning the authenticity of
Hunter Biden's laptop, October 19, 2020

*From what I've read and know, the intelligence
community warned [Trump] that Giuliani was
being fed disinformation from the Russians.
And we also know that Putin is trying very hard
to spread disinformation about Joe Biden.*

—President Joe Biden on *60
Minutes*, October 25, 2021

The hot new term on the right is "weaponization"—as in weaponization of government power centers in order to chill civil liberties. And not just government power centers, but other easily manipulated entities (e.g., social media platforms) that can be major influencers of public opinion.

Exhibit A of how dangerous the public-private chill machine can be is of course the now infamous multifaceted suppression campaign surrounding Hunter Biden's laptop from hell. Here, fifty-one former intelligence officials—with the knowledge of the FBI (we now know the FBI authenticated Hunter's laptop a year prior to the initial *New York Post* report), Facebook, and Twitter—worked as an emergency response team to minimize an unfolding scandal that post-election polls showed would have been a game changer on the eve of Election 2020.

That this all-star disinformation team was wildly successful in its suppression campaign is without doubt: Biden won, Trump lost. And major segments of blue America still believe Hunter's laptop was a Russian false-flag operation carried out to reelect President Trump.

Equally unsurprising has been the unrepentant attitude of the miscreants who cast aspersions on the authenticity of the laptop and the damning evidence contained therein. Indeed, contrition has never been a hallmark of the "get Trump" crowd. It was rather "anything goes for the cause."

THE BOTTOM LINE: I'm reminded of what former Senate Majority Leader Harry Reid said after it was revealed that he had lied about Mitt Romney's alleged failure to pay federal income taxes (for a decade) during the 2012 presidential campaign: "Romney didn't win, did he?"

RUSSIA, RUSSIA, RUSSIA

*Vice President Joe Biden and President
Obama knew about it. Hillary [Clinton]
fabricated it. The FBI orchestrated it.
And the mainstream media sold it.*

—U.S. Rep. Tom Tiffany (R-WI)
tweet, June 6, 2023

A lie told often enough becomes the truth.

—Vladimir Lenin

After six years of exhaustive media coverage, relentless investigation by congressional staff (on both sides of the aisle), and reports from Special Counsels Robert Mueller and John Durham, what was once a sensational theory about a presidential candidate (and sitting president) operating in conjunction with Vladimir Putin and Russian interests was revealed to be a…sophisticated, cynical hoax cobbled together by Hillary Clinton, members of the Democratic National Committee, and senior officials within the Department of Justice in order to mitigate the political damage resulting from Clinton's own email scandal.

This succinct quote from the third-term congressman from Wisconsin captures the entire delusory escapade in easy-to-understand language. But that second quote continues to haunt our politics.

**THE BOTTOM LINE: What looked ridiculous from the
jump turned out to be…ridiculous in the end.**

PRESIDENTIAL PAPERS

*Our laws that protect national defense
information are critical to the safety and security
of the United States and must be enforced.
Violations of those laws put our country at risk.*

—Special Counsel Jack Smith, June 9, 2023

Wherever the law is, crime can be found.

—Aleksandr Solzhenitsyn in
The Gulag Archipelago

On June 8, 2023, Joe Biden's Department of Justice (through specially appointed counsel Jack Smith) indicted former president Donald Trump for alleged willful mishandling of classified documents and related offenses including obstruction of justice and espionage. Here, a special counsel with particular expertise in *war crimes* prosecutions—appointed by Biden's attorney general Merrick Garland, who was previously denied a Supreme Court seat by a GOP-led Senate—indicted a former president and leading challenger to Biden's reelection.

That the news broke on the same day members of Congress gained access to an FBI document linking a $5 million payment from Burisma, the Ukrainian energy giant, to Hunter Biden was not viewed as particularly newsworthy by the mainstream media.

Notably, legal commentators focused on the inclusion of obstruction and espionage counts in the Trump indictment, possibly seeking to distinguish Trump's Mar-a-Lago documents from Biden's previously reported possession of classified documents found at the University of Delaware, the Penn Biden Center in D.C., and in a garage of the Biden family home in Wilmington, Delaware.

Commentators from the left and right saw the indictment as strong in light of the president's failure to return the classified documents (some of which bore markings indicating they were of extraordinary sensitivity, including intercepted signals intelligence—from other governments) upon repeated requests; subsequent conversations with Trump counsel wherein the former president allegedly suggested that not all requested documents be produced; and another conversation with staffers and two other individuals wherein Mr. Trump allegedly refers to secret documents that contain military attack plans against a foreign adversary (likely Iran).

Still, angst over the increasingly grotesque weaponization of federal law enforcement (see Solzhenitsyn's quote above) and the disparate treatment of similarly situated individuals (compare Hillary Clinton's email and classified documents scandal and Hunter Biden's long history of influence peddling) grew stronger in flyover America.

THE BOTTOM LINE: Repeated instances of disparate treatment may end up making the former president a more sympathetic figure in the eyes of the voting public. Wouldn't that be a kick in the pants for the Trump-hating media?!

CATHOLICS AND THE FBI

*[Suggest] the exploration of new avenues
for tripwire and source development
against traditional Catholics [including
those who favor the Latin mass].*

—FBI field memo targeting alleged
radicalization of traditional Catholic
churches (subsequently disavowed by FBI
Director Chris Wray and Attorney General
Merrick Garland), January 23, 2023

At first blush, it sounds crazy: The Biden Department of Justice looking to spy on American Catholics in the context of domestic terror investigations. Indeed, FBI Director Wray minimized the story in a July 17, 2023, response to Congress, assuring the American public that the report was limited to a Richmond, Virginia, field office—a one-off so to speak.

And then a subpoenaed memo produced to the House Judiciary Committee reflected two additional undercover operations (in Portland, Oregon, and in California) of congregations linked to the Society of Saint Pius X—founded in 1970 by a since-excommunicated (now deceased) priest. The discovery led Republican leaders to demand Director Wray revise his prior testimony.

On December 3, 2023, the FBI's narrative took on additional water when the House Judiciary Committee and its Select Committee on the Weaponization of the Federal Government issued a damning report on the Bureau's internal processes, concluding that the agency committed "errors at every step of the drafting, review, approval, and removal process of the memorandum."

Whether the genesis of the FBI surveillance was the well-publicized 2022 acquittal of a pro-life activist (Mark Houck) accused of assaulting a man accompanying a patient at a Philadelphia Planned Parenthood office remains unclear.

Yet another instance of the DOJ targeting highly protected speech—this time religious conviction. Dangerous but unsurprising ground for Mr. Biden's chief law enforcement agency.

THE BOTTOM LINE: The Catholic vote has become an increasingly important part of the GOP's political base. The Biden administration's heavy-handed approach to traditional Catholic churches can only serve to further energize suburban Catholic support for the GOP.

PSEUDONYMS

Robin Ware, Robert L. Peters, and JRB Ware.

—Pseudonyms used by Joe Biden in
communications with his son Hunter

The late August 2023 headlines screamed: "National Archives has 5,400 emails from Biden pseudonym accounts." Two months later, the same media outlets reported the emails covered 82,000 pages (sent and received).

Let that one sink in for a long minute. The sitting vice president of the United States utilized at least three different pseudonyms in order to disguise his identity when engaging in email exchanges, including with his son Hunter. And this against the "absolute wall" (per Joe Biden) that allegedly existed between Hunter's foreign business deals and himself.

And it all came to light because the Southeastern Legal Foundation filed a lawsuit after the National Archives failed to respond to a Freedom of Information Act request.

Former House Speaker Newt Gingrich asked how the archives could find material relevant to President Trump so quickly but could miss 5,400 emails from the vice president's archives. I think it was a rhetorical question.

THE BOTTOM LINE: I suppose there is a legitimate explanation for Vice President Biden's use of pseudonyms. I just can't think of any.

SPY AGENCIES

*Report: CIA Started Russian Collusion
Hoax by asking Foreign Governments
to Spy on Trump Campaign*

—*The Federalist*, February 13, 2024

Trump supporters and detractors alike recall the time CBS correspondent Leslie Stahl challenged President Trump's claim that the federal government was spying on his campaign during an ultra-contentious interview on *60 Minutes*.

The clip was run on a loop by anti-Trump media outlets as proof that the president was paranoid—that he lacked the mental acuity required for the most powerful position on earth. Alas, there was no apology forthcoming from Ms. Stahl or the fourth estate when *Public Substack* and reporters Michael

Shellenberger, Matt Taibbi, and Alex Gutentag reported (in February 2024) that CIA Director John Brennan had asked foreign intelligence services to surveil twenty-six Trump associates during the 2016 campaign, a task his agency was forbidden from performing as warrantless surveillance of U.S. citizens is prohibited by U.S. law. You will recall this is the same Mr. Brennan who was one of the fifty-one open letter signees that happily provided electoral cover for the Bidens when Hunter's laptop problem arose during the waning days of the 2020 campaign.

THE BOTTOM LINE: An uber-left political partisan occupying the top job at America's most important spy agency was an accident waiting to happen—and it did.

DE-BANKING

...viewpoint-based de-banking is on the rise....

—Jeremy Tedesco, Senior Counsel &
Senior Vice President of Corporate
Engagement, Alliance Defending Freedom

The weaponization of America's banking system is one of the more egregious consequences of the January 6, 2021 U.S. Capitol riot. Specifically, the ability of liberal interest groups to label conservative interest groups (i.e., pro-life, pro-gun, pro-fossil-fuel, pro-legal-immigration) as simply "pro-insurrectionist hate organizations" subject to potential loss of banking privileges.

Such was the case as leftist organizations developed lists of right-leaning groups for referral to an all-too-willing federal bureaucracy—and an all-too-willing banking sector—happy to target businesses and people with opinions adverse to progressive causes. Per an investigation by the House Judiciary Select Subcommittee on the Weaponization of the Federal Government, right-leaning interest groups such as the Family Research Council, Pacific Justice Institute, and Federation for American Immigration Reform came in for the special treatment.

The Select Subcommittee pinpointed a 2020 report by two left-wing advocacy groups (Institute for Strategic Dialogue and the Global Disinformation Index) as the baseline source utilized by Biden's Treasury Department to notify the world's leading financial institutions of the alleged right-wing miscreants, a process that became even more pronounced after January 6th.

> **THE BOTTOM LINE: De-banking pressure that targets right-wing organizations is an especially nefarious misuse of federal power. The chilling of free speech and the limitation of consumer choice are, of course, two primary biproducts. There is seemingly no end to the ways and means of Biden-era censorship.**

ROCK BOTTOM FOR MEDIA, INC.

Trump says there will be a "blood bath" if he loses the election.

—NBC News, March 16, 2024

- Trump as Russian Asset

- The "Wuhan Virus" / Wet Market

- Nick Sandmann / Covington Catholic High School

- "Mostly peaceful protests"

- Trump Tower Meeting with Russian Lawyer

- Kyle Rittenhouse / Kenosha, Wisconsin

- Intel Agencies Did Not Spy on Trump Campaign

- Jussie Smollett / MAGA

- "Very fine people" / Charlottesville, Virginia

- Russia, Russia, Russia / Mueller Report

- Trump Hid Hush Money Paid to Stormy Daniels

- Hunter's Laptop

- Hunter's Benign Business Model

- "Blood Bath"

Think about these major Trump-era storylines. All were given breathless, front-page coverage. All became generally accepted articles of faith in the short term. All were subsequently proven to be either seriously flawed, taken out of context, or simply untrue. And all have been allowed to linger in the public consciousness.

This spate of invented, embellished, misreported media stories is indeed alarming, but not surprising. The media's lack of objectivity when it comes to anything and everything Trump will not change. Only an Elon Musk-led Twitter and some GOP-led congressional oversight hearings have been able to blunt at least some of the damage. Only another Trump victory will finally degrade the most outlandish of them.

THE BOTTOM LINE: Republican and right-leaning candidates have long found themselves on the short end of mainstream media's political reporting, but it took one Donald J. Trump to fully expose its utter shamelessness.

MISDEMEANORS…AND LAWFARE

Just because you're paranoid doesn't
mean everyone is not out to get you.

—Humorist Joseph Heller

True: On April 4, 2023, Manhattan District Attorney Alvin Bragg brought a thirty-four-count indictment against President Donald J. Trump in the so-called Stormy Daniels hush money case.

Also true: Bragg's predecessor, Cyrus R. Vance, had previously declined to bring misdemeanor criminal charges on the same evidence.

Also true: Vance's office appears to have dropped its investigation into the Trump hush money matter during the summer of 2019.

Also true: In 2021, federal prosecutor Matthew Colangelo (who had left his previous position as the number three official in the Biden Justice Department) joined Bragg's staff in New York.

Also true: Colangelo replaced two assistant district attorneys who had resigned because the investigation into Trump had not progressed to their satisfaction.

Also true: Mr. Colangelo had previous experience in the New York Attorney General's office wherein he had led investigations into the Trump Foundation and civil fraud case (presently on appeal).

Also true: Mr. Colangelo was paid $12,000 by the Democratic National Committee for "political consulting" in 2018.

Also true: The trial judge's daughter, Loren Merchan, is a Democrat consultant whose clients used the Trump trial to raise tens of millions of dollars on behalf of their campaigns.

Also true: Trump's former attorney, Michael Cohen, was the prosecution's star witness in the case.

Also true: In the run-up to election day in 2016, Cohen paid Daniels to keep quiet about an alleged affair with Trump out of a shell corporation he created and funded.

Also true: Cohen was subsequently reimbursed by the Trump organization for "legal services," and the entry was made on the corporate books.

Also true: Bragg charged Trump with falsely filing a business expense—a misdemeanor that carries a two-year statute of limitations in New York.

Also true: The trial produced no evidence that Trump even knew how the payments were recorded on the corporate books.

Also true: Per commentator Jonathan Turley, Cohen made the pitch to the jury that they should put his former client in jail for following his own legal advice.

Also true: Only during the trial did the public (kinda) find out Bragg's theory of the case: that the hush money payment and recordation was committed in furtherance of a conspiracy to promote political candidates by "unlawful means" under New York law—*even though the payments were not recorded until after the election was over.*

Also true: The jury was allowed to choose from three possible other crimes, including an illegal campaign contribution, falsification of a bank record, or a tax violation, to further the unlawful means utilized to carry out the conspiracy.

Also true: The former chair of the Federal Election Commission, Brad Smith, opined that the payment to Daniels was not a campaign expense.

Also true: Brad Smith was not allowed to testify at trial.

THE BOTTOM LINE: A long-dead misdemeanor allegedly used to cover for an unprosecuted federal campaign violation, a salacious description of a supposed hookup from eighteen years ago, a deep blue judge and team of prosecutors, a credibility-challenged and disbarred former counsel with an axe to grind, and a gag order placed on the leading contender for the presidency—all of these had the pundits, media types, and regular ol' folks scratching their heads. What "crime" were Messrs. Trump and Cohen attempting to conceal by recording $130,000 worth of payments as legal fees in consideration of a perfectly legal non-disclosure agreement?

ALL ABOUT THE CHILDREN

*Here's why Biden's bleeding support
among black and young Americans.*

—Adam Coleman, *New York Post*,
November 6, 2023

As polls continued to reflect a startling loss of support for Biden's reelection among young people, the federal government was further weaponized in order to stop the bleeding.

New and ever more aggressive attempts to achieve student debt forgiveness were made, no limit abortion rights (again) became central to campaign talking points, the administration announced plans to federally reschedule cannabis thereby easing restrictions on marijuana use nationwide, and hardly a mention was made (let alone condemnation) of ongoing pro-Palestinian/Hamas demonstrations at college commencements.

THE BOTTOM LINE: This time, appeals to more liberal-minded young people will likely fail. Recall this is the COVID-19 generation that had a ringside seat to really big government repeatedly making really bad decisions—even when "the science" dictated otherwise. Accordingly, and contrary to the entire woke narrative, this may end up being the most conservative generation since Reagan. Wouldn't that be a kick in the pants?

EPILOGUE

And so here we are—two editions and 142 reasons later—left with the question of how to place an appropriate wrap on the Biden era. My best answer to that question follows.

To wit: six-term U.S. *Senator* Joe Biden would be unrecognizable to *President* Joe Biden. The former defined eastern mainstream liberalism for forty years; the latter constantly is chomping at the bit to implement the latest experiment from the progressive left's handbook. One was content to take care of Delaware-based credit-card-issuing big banks, while the other hands out a blizzard of job-defeating regulations, tax increases, and uber-leftist class and race rhetoric.

Whether as a function of declining mental capacity or a late-life conversion to the woke religion, the forty-sixth president led a unique effort to federalize and weaponize government power. The reach was seemingly limitless, from net neutrality to voting rights to gun rights to land use to COVID-19 lockdowns to free speech under the First Amendment. As a result, federal law enforcement and the Department of Justice were politicized to an extent unheard of just a few years ago.

Domestically, consumer goods and services are far more expensive than four years ago. Biden's expansionary fiscal policy has spurred prolonged inflation far beyond the short-term spike that voters were promised. Interest rates have accordingly risen, leading to a housing slowdown and sense of malaise among young people looking to afford a mortgage at reasonable rates. To boot: a recent slowdown in growth has rekindled fears of stagflation, an unwelcome Jimmy Carter–era malady.

On foreign policy, Mr. Biden has combined the worst instincts of the "Blame America First" crowd with the Obama era's indulgence towards the world's most malicious regimes. The depressing results are obvious: Russia, China, and Iran grew stronger and closer while a war-weary Europe grows weaker and ever more dependent on Russian oil. Add the catastrophic withdrawal from Afghanistan and the re-emergence of the Taliban as a regional threat, and a picture of dangerous and provocative failure emerges.

Some readers of this tome love Donald J. Trump. Others are more lukewarm in their assessment. Still others remain uncomfortable with the always cage-rattling Donald. Be that as it may, America now faces a binary decision: Trump or Biden. We can choose either robust—or another four years of weak, woke, and wobbly.

I pray we make the right decision.

I was blessed with two loving parents, Bob and Nancy Ehrlich, who succeeded in giving their only son everything when everything was almost beyond their reach. I was blessed with a true partner in every aspect of my career and every season of life with my wife, Kendel. I am blessed with two sons, Drew and Josh, who remain our most hopeful reflections on the world and continue to make us beyond proud. I am blessed with the long-standing friendship and support of Bob and Elaine Pevenstein and the tutelage of Dr. Richard Vatz, who has always been my invaluable political barometer. I am blessed with Chris Massoni, my longtime aide—and her husband, Greg Massoni, my confidante and brother from another mother whom I count among so many unconditional friends and loyal supporters who have been by our side in celebration and sorrow. By any measure, I am a rich man…

As in my print and online columns and my previous five books, my writing is my own. Through what I have learned in the decades of my political and professional careers, along with my discernment of world events, both past and present, I have accrued almost a lifetime of knowledge and observations—at least six books and hundreds of opinion columns worth!

So, dear reader, thank you for your interest in what I have to say. And thank you for paying attention to what a short almost four years of chaos and dysfunction in government has done to our way of life and to our standing around the world.

Now the rest is up to you. Absorb the messages contained herein and spread the word that the reputation of our democracy is in need of restoration, and the strength of our republic is in need of rebuilding. The most powerful rebuttal to the wildly successful "Us and Them" strategy that has (by design) divided our nation is a resounding return to sound leadership at every level of government. It is our only hope. It can be done, and frankly, it *must* be done if the United States of America is to exist as we know it beyond our generation. Just as the courageous framers of the Constitution paid it forward for us, we owe it to those Americans still to come to do the hard things. Just look at what a roomful of patriots were able to do!

Photo by *The Baltimore Sun*

Governor Robert L. Ehrlich is a graduate of Princeton University and Wake Forest University School of Law and is a former governor of Maryland as well as a former United States congressman and state legislator.

He is the author of *Turn This Car Around: The Roadmap to Restoring America, America: Hope for Change, Turning Point: Picking Up the Pieces after Eight Years of Failed Progressive Policies, Bet You Didn't See that One Coming: Obama, Trump, and the End of Washington's Regular Order,* and *Original, Unconventional & Inconvenient: Donald J. Trump and His MAGA Movement,* in addition to columns and opinion pieces that have appeared in America's leading newspapers and periodicals, including *The Washington Examiner*, *The Washington Post*, *The Baltimore Sun*, *The Washington Times*, *The Weekly Standard*, *National Review*, *Western Journal* online, and *The Daily Caller*.

Governor Ehrlich is counsel at the international law firm of King & Spalding in Washington, DC, and lives with his wife, Kendel, and their children, Drew and Josh, in Annapolis, Maryland.

www.ingramcontent.com/pod-product-compliance
Ingram Content Group UK Ltd.
Pitfield, Milton Keynes, MK11 3LW, UK
UKHW021702190726
13853UKWH00001B/399